CW00546018

THE COLLECTED POEMS OF
Charles Hamilton
SORLEY

Books by Jean Moorcroft Wilson

ISAAC ROSENBERG, POET AND PAINTER

I WAS AN ENGLISH POET: A CRITICAL BIOGRAPHY OF
SIR WILLIAM WATSON

CHARLES HAMILTON SORLEY, A BIOGRAPHY

THE COLLECTED POEMS OF
Charles Hamilton
SORLEY

Edited by
Jean Moorcroft Wilson

CECIL WOOLF · LONDON

First published 1985
© 1985 Jean Moorcroft Wilson

Cecil Woolf Publishers, 1 Mornington Place, London NW1 7RP
Tel: 01-387 2394

British Library Cataloguing in Publication Data
Sorley, Charles Hamilton
The collected poems of Charles Hamilton Sorley.
I. Title   II. Wilson, Jean Moorcroft
821'.912   PR6037.07
ISBN 0-900821-53-1

Contents

Endpapers: 'Sorley's Signpost', from a watercolour by his nephew, Julian Bickersteth, 1938. Courtesy of Miss Ursula Bickersteth.

Introduction

Charles Hamilton Sorley is probably the last of the First
World War poets not to have received full recognition,
though an increasing number of writers have acknowledg-
ed his interest. Yet Sorley occupies a unique position
among these poets. Chronologically he fits in with the
early somewhat idealistic poets such as Brooke and Gren-
fell: he joined up at the first possible opportunity and
was killed a year later in October 1915. Yet philosophically
he is far closer to later, grimmer, more disillusioned poets
such as Owen, Sassoon and Rosenberg. Without their
experience of the horrors of the Somme Sorley could
nevertheless see through the heroic ideal:

> Such, such is Death: no triumph: no defeat:
> Only an empty pail, a slate rubbed clean,
> A merciful putting away of what has been.

When he wrote this poem Sorley had had no direct
experience of fighting. What delights and surprises one
about Sorley is his maturity of thought, his down-to-earth
approach to highly emotive subjects. 'When you see
millions of the mouthless dead / Across your dreams in
pale battalions go' he tells his reader, 'Say not soft things
as other men have said, / That you'll remember. For you
need not so'. Yet it is not cynicism which dictates such
sentiments so early in the war. It is rather a sense of
detachment brought about partly by birth and partly by
circumstance. For Sorley was a Scot and said himself

that he had no real sense of patriotism towards England, though he felt obliged to fight for her. In fact his first feelings of patriotism were ironically towards Germany, where he had been studying just before the outbreak of war. He was on a walk with his German landlady in February 1914 when he heard some German soldiers singing 'something glorious and senseless about the Fatherland':

And when I got home, I felt I was a German, and proud to be a German: when the tempest of the singing was at its loudest, I felt that perhaps I could die for Deutschland — and I have never had an inkling of that feeling about England, and never shall.

Still, as he went on to say, the feeling died with the cessation of the singing, while the real affection and admiration he had acquired for the Germans over his seven months stay continued even after they became 'the enemy'. So that he could see both sides of the question far more clearly than the average soldier. The Germans, he writes to his ex-headmaster, 'are a splendid lot and I wish the silly papers would realize that they are fighting for a principle just as much as we are'. His sympathy for Germany makes him more objective than most of his fellow-countrymen, as this letter to his school friend Hopkinson shows:

. . . it seems to me that Germany's only fault . . . is a lack of insight and sympathy with those who differ from her. We are not fighting a bully, but a bigot. They are a young nation and don't yet see that what they consider is being done for the good of the world may be really being done for self-gratification . . . I regard the war as one between sisters, between Martha and Mary, the efficient and intolerant, against the casual and sympathetic. Each side has a virtue for which it is fighting, and each that virtue's supplementary vice. And I hope that whatever the material result of the conflict, it will purge these two virtues of their vices, and efficiency and tolerance will no longer be incompatible.

However sympathetic Sorley is towards Germany he realizes that he must choose between the two countries and he has no hesitation: 'But I think that tolerance is the larger virtue of the two, and efficiency must be her servant. So I am quite glad to fight this rebellious servant'.

In spite of his decision and because of his conflicting feelings about Germany and England Sorley is very critical of anything that smacks of 'jingoism': 'England— I am sick of the sound of the word. In training to fight for England, I am training to fight for that deliberate hypocrisy, that terrible middle-class sloth of outlook and appalling "imaginative indolence" that has marked us out from generation to generation . . .' He is particularly critical of this attitude in Rupert Brooke, whose earlier work he admired. Sorley's letter to his mother about Brooke's death in April 1915 pinpoints the difference between the two poets:

That last sonnet-sequence of his, of which you sent me the review in the *Times Lit. Sup.*, and which has been so praised, I find (with the exception of that beginning 'These hearts were woven of human joys and cares, Washed marvellously with sorrow' which is not about himself) overpraised. He is far too obsessed with his own sacrifice regarding the going to war of himself (and others) as a highly intense, remarkable and sacrificial exploit, whereas it is merely the conduct demanded of him (and others) by the turn of circumstances, where the non-compliance with this demand would have made life intolerable. It was not that "they" gave up anything of that list he gives in one sonnet: but that the essence of these things had been endangered by circumstances over which he had no control and he must fight to recapture them. He has clothed his attitude in fine words: but he has taken the sentimental attitude.

Sorley's own attitude was far from sentimental. He fought willingly for his country, but he did so with his eyes open. Coming so early in the war his attitude gives him, quite apart from his intrinsic merits as a writer, a strong historic interest. He also provides a link between the early and later poets, who have usually been seen as two distinct groups.

It may help us to understand Sorley's position more clearly if we look more closely at his life. Charles Hamilton was born in Aberdeen on 19 May 1895, the elder twin son of Professor William Ritchie Sorley and his wife, Janetta Colquhoun Smith. Both parents were of Lowland descent and Charles was proud of his Scottish origin. It did, as we have seen, make him feel rather detached from the English, whom he regarded almost as another race. Both sides of his family contained a number of writers and religious thinkers, as well as a plentiful share of strong-minded individualists, all of which helps us to understand Sorley's own character. His father, during his distinguished career in moral philosophy. produced at least eight books and numerous papers, as well as contributing chapters to *The Cambridge History of English Literature.* His son inherited both his literary ability and his philosophic leanings. Sorley's mother, who was well-educated and independently-minded for her day, wrote a book about Cambridge University, *King's Daughters* (1937) and also the introduction to Charles's Letters after his death. Her son resembled her in his lively manner and insatiable curiosity. His elder sister Jean, whom I met in her eighties, was a highly articulate, intelligent and cultured person who obviously reflected the family background.

Charles's twin, Kenneth, provides more of a puzzle. The weaker, less able of the two, he made Charles feel guilty at times at his own easy successes. He had an almost apologetic attitude towards those less fortunate: 'I often feel terribly unworthy and untried,' he wrote in 1915, 'in that life has given me no troubles or difficulties at home, such as alone strengthen a man'. Kenneth's problems at school, which were accentuated by his twin's lack of them, probably accounts for Charles's awareness of and sympathy with the failures, expressed so clearly in his 'Tale of Two Careers'.

Charles had been born in a quite ordinary house in Don Street in Old Aberdeen, but in 1896, a year after his birth, the family moved to Powis House, a splendid Adam mansion standing high above the Old Town. It was, according to his mother, a 'fine windy place and a good natural nursery for children'. It is no coincidence that Charles in later life preferred the wilder elements of nature, wind and rain, to its gentler aspects, which seemed to him stagnant and suffocating. By analogy he preferred fierce pagan life to Christianity: 'Give me *The Odyssey* and I return the New Testament to store'. It was this Scott-like landscape which indirectly started Sorley on his literary career, though in a very modest way. Inspired by Bella Sidney Woolf's *All in a Castle Fair*, which took place in a similarly romantic setting, Charles, Kenneth and Jean began to invent their own saga, rather like the young Brontës. Since the twins were well under five, however, the episodes were not committed to paper, but were related to their mother.

Charles's first independent effort at writing came after the family left Scotland for Cambridge in 1900, when Professor Sorley succeeded Sidgwick as Knightbridge Professor of Moral Philosophy and became a fellow of King's. Intoxicated by the lays of Scott and Macaulay, whom his mother had taught him to love, Charles began to write long epic poems of a similar nature. His mother obviously believed poetry was an important part of their early education, which she had herself undertaken, for she writes:

> Their education, besides the acquisition of an angular handwriting, consisted chiefly in singing and marching games in French and English, history stories and fairy stories, reading aloud from the Bible and the *Pilgrim's Progress*, but especially in learning by heart any amount of poetry—ballads and passages of Shake-

speare, Walter Scott, Macaulay and Blake.

When the twins were nine Mrs Sorley had, regretfully, to send them to school and King's College Choir School was the natural choice. Charles did badly to begin with, but when English was accepted in the timetable as a respectable academic subject then he began to do well in at least one subject. His general performance improved noticeably in his last two terms, when he was again top in English, winning both a prize for the subject and a scholarship to Marlborough College.

The same tendency to do very well at what interested him and badly at what bored him marked Sorley's career at Marlborough. He still enjoyed his English lessons enormously, though he made life difficult for his English teacher with his high spirits. Classics, German and maths he disliked, and performed accordingly. Games and even the O.T.C. interested him enough to win his enthusiastic participation. But he was always something of a rebel and this showed itself in his rejection of orthodox Christianity at the age of eighteen. It also showed itself in his refusal to try for the Indian Civil Service, as his parents wished. He was far more interested in becoming a social worker and at one point, after a violent disagreement with his classics teacher, Atkey, threatened to leave Marlborough early to become an Elementary School teacher. His music master, Dyson, not himself an Oxbridge man as Sorley was quick to point out, cleverly persuaded him to take a degree so that he could teach in a working man's college or night-school. Once he had agreed to that Sorley had no difficulty in settling down to work and in his final term won yet another scholarship—to University College, Oxford.

Sorley loved Marlborough, but more for its surrounding countryside than for the school itself. His favourite pursuit was cross-country running in the rain, when all the wildness and primitive history of the downs gave him a mystical sense of belonging to the earth: 'The earth even more than Christ,' he told a friend, 'is the ultimate ideal of what man should strive to be.' This revelation seems to have inspired him to start writing poetry in earnest and one of his first efforts is an attempt to explain his experience more fully:

> When the rain is coming down,
> And all Court is still and bare,
> And the leaves fall wrinkled, brown,
> Through the kindly winter air,
> And in tattered flannels I
> 'Sweat' beneath a tearful sky,
> And the sky is dim and grey,
> And the rain is coming down,
> And I wander far away
> From the little red-capped town:
> There is something in the rain
> That would bid me to remain:
> There is something in the wind
> That would whisper, 'Leave behind
> All this land of time and rules,
> Land of bells and early schools.
> Latin, Greek and College food
> Do you precious little good.
> Leave them: if you would be free
> Follow, follow, after me!'

In spite of his great love of the downs and his increasing affection for the school, Sorley decided to leave Marlborough early, mainly because he felt life was becoming too easy and he was always suspicious of ease:

> When one reaches the top of a public school, one has such unbounded opportunities of getting unbearably conceited that I don't see how anyone survives the change that must come when the tin god is swept off his little Kingdom and becomes an unimportant mortal again. And besides I am sure it is far too enjoyable, and one is awfully tempted to pose all the time and be theatrical.

Having won his scholarship in December 1913, he had the choice of spending his last two terms elsewhere. So, encouraged by his parents, he decided to spend them in Germany, learning something about the language and the literature. It was an ironic choice in view of the impending war.

At Schwerin in Mecklenberg Sorley discovered a language and a people. He also experienced for the first time the pleasures of independence. It was as a person rather than a poet that he developed, though there is a noticeable increase in the maturity of his work afterwards. Professor Sorley had chosen the quiet provincial town of Schwerin in northern Germany as a safe place for his son to start learning independence. The family chosen was also ostensibly safe—a lawyer, Herr Doktor Beutin and his wife, who was to give Sorley lessons. No one could have predicted that Frau Beutin would become rather too fond of her handsome eighteen-year old lodger and he of her. She was a lonely, childless middle-aged housewife, who had become overwrought in her isolation and frustrated by her lack of outlet for her artistic yearnings. Sorley was by nature sympathetic, especially towards those who were unfulfilled. He was also grateful to the Frau for introducing him to the 'glorious' German language in which they had read so much romantic literature together. Away from his family and friends he turned to her for friendship. Yet it is highly unlikely that either of them was conscious of how far their relationship had developed, though Sorley afterwards recognised in her 'an unsatisfied maternal instinct'. So mature in many ways, Sorley was almost completely inexperienced when it came to women. He was to remain so to the end of his life.

No less fascinating to Sorley in Schwerin was his discovery of Goethe, whom he started to read in the original. He also became interested in drama when he saw several Ibsen plays performed in translation at the local theatre. More lightheartedly he began to enjoy hockey as he had never enjoyed it at Marlborough, where it was taken too seriously for his liking. The Schwerin hockey-players also provoked him into reading *The Odyssey* out of shame at his own ignorance. He admired their genuine love of learning, which again contrasted sharply with Marlborough students.

Most importantly of all, by the end of his three-month stay in Schwerin Sorley had begun to feel truly independent and this was consolidated by his further three months at Jena, the then German equivalent of Oxford or Cambridge. Here Sorley lived entirely alone in a tiny bedsitter, chose his own lectures from the university programme, joined some societies and made friends among the German students. He continued to read Greek, studied a little philosophy and played more than a little tennis. A performance of *A Midsummer Night's Dream* in the Thuringian forest convinced him that Shakespeare was as great if not greater than his newest 'prophet' Goethe. Sorley had blamed Goethe for what he regarded as a 'drying-up' of his creative instincts and in Jena he produced no more poetry than in Schwerin, though from both places he sent long, witty, beautifully observed letters which show him developing as a prose writer if not as a poet.

It was while Sorley was still in Germany, just setting off on a walking tour of the Moselle valley with his school friend, Arthur Hopkinson, that Austria at last declared war on Serbia. Sorley had watched the tension rise in Jena, and it is highly likely that he had received his father's letter ordering him to return home, but with the untried daring of youth he set off on his trip with 'Hopper' at the end of July. On August 1st it was brought to an abrupt end in Neumagen, when the two boys heard that England had joined in the war on the opposite side. And in Trier the next day, where they gave themselves up to the police, they were arrested and put in prison for eight hours—all of which Sorley seems to have enjoyed. When he eventually arrived back in Cambridge, after still more adventures, he joined up at the first possible opportunity. His sympathies were still very much with the Germans. He felt they must be fought, as we have seen, but the situation made him 'helplessly angry', as he put it. 'But isn't all this bloody?' he wrote to Hutchinson, a few days after his safe arrival in

Cambridge. 'I am full of mute and burning rage and annoyance and sulkiness about it. I could wager that out of twelve million eventual combatants there aren't twelve who really want it.'

At the end of August Sorley was gazetted as a temporary 2nd Lieutenant in the Seventh Battalion—the first of the new 'service' battalions—of the Suffolk Regiment. The same day he left for a training camp at Churn in Berkshire and a month later joined his battalion at Shorncliffe near Folkestone. As the months passed he became increasingly bored and disillusioned. 'The monotony of this existence is alarming, and on the increase', he tells his brother Kenneth, who is at Oxford, early in 1915:

> Officers and men are both suffering equally from staleness. We don't look like removing for a long time yet on account of our supposed inefficiency. So the passage of days is swift, and nothing to show for it. Somehow one never lives in the future now, only in the past, which is apt to be morbid and begins to make one like an old man. The war is a chasm in time. I do wish that all journalists etc., who say that war is an ennobling purge etc., etc., could be muzzled. It simply makes people unhappy and uncomfortable, if that is a good thing. All illusions about the splendour of war will, I hope, be gone after the war.

In spite of, perhaps even because of, the tedium of his existence, Sorley starts to write poetry again and continues to do so when his division finally arrives in France at the end of May 1915.

Sorley was at first highly stimulated by the change of circumstances, particularly by the idyllic surroundings in which he found himself:

> But this is perfect [he wrote to a friend]. The other officers have heard the heavy guns and perhaps I shall soon. They make perfect cider in this valley: still, like them. There are clouds of dust along the roads, and in the leaves: but the dust here is native and caressing and pure, not like the dust of Aldershot, gritted and fouled by motors and thousands of feet. 'Tis a very Limbo lake: set between the tireless railways behind and twenty miles in front the fighting. Drink its cider and paddle in its rushy streams: and see if you care whether you die tomorrow?

Co-existing with this sense of tranquility is Sorley's consciousness of danger and death. Although living in almost complete isolation from the rest of the battalion among quiet fields, he knows that he will soon have to leave for the front. Not surprisingly the two sonnets he manages to write during this lull reflect his preoccupation with death and the coming struggle. It was something of a relief to him when his battalion finally took over a new system of trenches near Ploegsteert. Here at last was some action, though mainly of the skirmishing variety. On one of these skirmishes, a night raid planned and led by Sorley himself, he showed his ability to face danger and death by crawling out after a soldier who had dropped his grenade and dragging him into the nearest shell-hole. Typically he made very little of the incident and his parents heard of it only through a fellow-officer.

Whether as a direct result of this incident or not, Sorley was promoted to Captain at the end of August, which meant that his leave was changed from mid-September to mid-October. By the time it fell due, however, he was no longer alive to take it, for he was killed on 13th October in the Battle of Loos. His battalion had been moved south to take the Hairpin trench near Hulluch and Sorley was shot in the head whilst taking over D Company for its wounded commander. His head fell gently forward on the sandbag he had been adjusting and those beside him could scarcely believe he was dead. The manner of his death was in keeping with his unromantic view of war.

One question which immediately suggests itself in relation to Sorley's life is why he turned to poetry at all. None of his immediate family or ancestors wrote poetry, though a number wrote prose. None of his friends chose verse as their medium. In fact, as Sorley himself remarked, writing poetry was looked upon with some suspicion in English public schools. Unlike many young poets, such as Rosenberg and Sassoon, he was not miserable or isolated as a child and thus forced back upon himself. On the contrary he seems to have been in almost every situation happy and well-adjusted. Yet from his earliest years he wrote as though he had no choice. This puzzled and pleased his family, who wanted to publish some of his poems privately in June 1915. But publication does not seem to have been nearly as important to Sorley as the writing itself and he put them off, referring to his own talents as of the 'small-holdings type'. He wrote because he had something he wanted to say, rather than as a self-conscious aesthete who thought it 'interesting'— a pose which his fellow-schoolboys and soldiers would have discouraged in any case. There are one or two exceptions among his juvenilia, where he seems to be experimenting with verse for verse's sake, but in each case they are inferior productions.

The development of Sorley's poetry from his earliest epic lays in the manner of Scott and Macaulay and his first published work 'The Tempest' at the age of ten, through his Marlborough poems to his war poems is relatively easy to trace. It is, as with many young poets, a process of falling under different influences, learning a little from each in turn, then finally rejecting their models as they find their own voice. Sorley's first Marlborough poems show such diverse influences as Coleridge, Shakespeare, Robert Louis Stevenson, Wordsworth, Kipling, Browning and Tennyson. It was not until he rejected the many in favour of one 'prophet' as he calls him that his poetry makes much impression. Meredith was his first choice in the attempt to free himself from the Tennysonian tradition. Meredith was quickly usurped by Masefield, whose desire to write poetry 'for the people' in simple language that they could understand appealed to Sorley's youthful rebelliousness against the 'establishment' in church, school and society. His allegiance to Masefield either provoked or fitted in with his rejection of such 'aesthetes' as Pater, whose 'fine' writing he despised. Predictably, he preferred austere poets like Hardy and Housman, equating, it would seem, sincerity with absence of flourish. This deep-rooted suspicion of ornament is almost certainly related to the puritanism which underlies his character.

Sorley's worship of Masefield was a necessary step in working himself free from the Tennysonian tradition, which persisted well into the twentieth century, and in this he resembles the Georgian poets. It was, however, an unconscious resemblance since he had read only the first volume of *Georgian Poetry*. Though he admired Abercrombie, de la Mare and Gibson, he was not influenced by them to any extent and even Masefield was 'shunted into a siding' when he left Marlborough. The works which follow, after a break of eight months in which he wrote only two poems, are free of any dominating influence. This is one reason why his war poems are in most respects his best. They also reflect the greater maturity he had acquired through being on his own in a foreign country without the protection of school or home. Finally, the war which brought with it the even greater responsibility of being an officer and the daily possibility of death, wound Sorley up to his highest pitch. The results are as stark and uncompromising as the life he was living.

Sorley's earliest surviving attempt at poetry, 'The Tempest' shows him already interested in what was to become one of his recurring themes, that is, the revelation of God through wind and rain. However, his next surviving verses are very different and rather disappointing. They are a group of occasional verses written mainly for and about school, such as 'Verses for a C1 House Concert', 'Rain' (though this also deals with his favourite theme), 'A Tale of Two Careers', a verse letter to the editor of *The Marlburian* and parts of 'A Call to Action'. The main part of 'A Call to Action' brings out another aspect of Sorley's work at this time, which might make one stop reading altogether: that is the highly moral or religious preaching to be found in 'Peace', 'Expectans Expectavi' and 'The Seekers'. Fortunately this pious phase passes quickly and his next poems revert to his obsession with the wilder aspects of nature. Running parallel with this and just as importantly for Sorley is the history it both conceals and reveals. Both interests emerge in works such as 'Barbury Camp', 'Rooks' I and II, 'Stones' and 'Return'. However, Sorley's most perfect expression of his mystical sense of oneness with nature is expressed in a poem he wrote about the Marlborough Downs after he left them, entitled 'Marlborough'.

The same sense of affinity with the earth is evident in the first of what can be loosely called Sorley's war poems, 'All the Hills and Vales Along', which his father believed was written at the outbreak of war. However it is also clear from this poem that war has tempered Sorley's pantheism with irony, for how is it possible otherwise to tell his 'marching men' 'So be merry, so be dead'. They may well return to the earth when they die, but they can hardly be expected to rejoice quite as straightforwardly as the poem at first seems to suggest. Sorley's ambivalent attitude towards death continues until his own death just over a year later. During this time he wrote fifteen poems, not including his verse epistle 'I have not brought my Odyssey'. Only six are directly concerned with war though the other nine are obviously inspired by his experience of army life in England and France. These nine suggest a strong sense of insecurity, a feeling of someone both waiting and

23

searching for answers to a bewildering situation.*

Sorley's confidence appears to return when he faces war directly and his poetry reflects this. Apart from 'To Germany', where he reveals his own conflict of loyalties, and his epitaph on a friend, there are four 'war' poems. The first, 'A Hundred Thousand Million Mites We Go', written in September 1914, shows an amazing insight into the horrors of war even before these were fully revealed. Opening with a startling and nightmarish image symbolising the complete insignificance of man in the holocaust, the poem is filled with a sense of desolation and bewilderment and ends with the same powerful image which opened it:

> A hundred thousand million mites we go
> Wheeling and tacking o'er the eternal plain,
> Some black with death — and some are white with woe.
> Who sent us forth? Who takes us home again?
>
> And there is sound of hymns of praise — to whom?
> And curses — on whom curses? — snap the air.
> And there is hope goes hand in hand with gloom,
> And blood and indignation and despair.

---

*'I yearned . . . I trod unpeopled spaces . . . I wander unfulfilled' ('Brand'): 'We are the homeless' ('To Poets'): 'Man only does not cease / From Striving and from cry' ('If I have suffered pain'): 'Blind, patient, hungry, hopeless . . . Unheard, unnamed, unnoticed, crucified / To our unutterable faith, we wait' ('Whom Therefore We Ignorantly Worship'): 'We sought / Full many stars in many skies to see' ('Deus Loquitur'): 'Across my past imaginings / Has dropped a blindness silent and slow' ('Lost').

And there is murmuring of the multitude
And blindness and great blindness, until some
Step forth and challenge blind Vicissitude
Who tramples on them: so that fewer come.

And nations, ankle-deep in love or hate,
Throw darts or kisses all the unwitting hour
Beside the ominous unseen tide of fate;
And there is emptiness and drink and power.

And some are mounted on swift steeds of thought
And some drag sluggish feet of stable toil.
Yet all, as though they furiously sought,
Twist turn and tussle, close and cling and coil.

A hundred thousand million mites we sway
Writhing and tossing on the eternal plain,
Some black with death—but most are bright with Day!
Who sent us forth? Who brings us home again?

The simplicity of the stanza form is matched here by
the directness of the imagery—black, white, blindness,
hymns, curses, swift steeds and bright Day. These rather
crude images which are not developed suggest the poet
feels this is no time for subtleties or sophistications.
Sorley is describing his apocalyptic vision of man's situation in life which is not dissimilar to Shelley's half-
despairing, half-hopeful picture in *The Triumph of Life.*
Like Shelley Sorley has no answers to his own bewildered
questions, though he seems to see some hope in the last
stanza, where 'white with woe' is transformed to 'bright
with Day'. At the same time this phrase adds to the

sense of tragedy implicit in the probable deaths of millions of fresh young men in war. The circular movement of the poem, which closes with a repetition of the opening stanza in a slightly varied form, underlines the sense of desperate, pointless movement, for in the end we seem to be back where we started. This frantic yet hopeless activity is also emphasized by the abrupt, broken rhythms and heavy alliteration of such lines as 'Twist, turn and tussle, close and cling and coil'. It is evident that Sorley was suspicious of the subjective approach; he seems to feel that the excessive emotions aroused by war must be controlled by a more objective, impersonal approach to the subject. So he distances himself and his reader from the actual physical experience and everyday details, concentrating instead on more abstract but no less powerful realities.

Sorley spent the next nine months waiting to face death. When his division was finally sent out to France at the end of May 1915 he felt death was becoming more real and wrote two more 'war' poems on the theme. And for this highly emotional subject he chooses the sonnet, one of the most disciplined of forms. The first of these 'Two Sonnets' is divided quite conventionally into an octet, in which he sets out and develops his theme through the image of that same signpost he used earlier in 'Le Revenant'. He extends this image in the sestet to an unexpected conclusion—that in some ways he looks forward to death as an adventure:

> Saints have adored the lofty soul of you.
> Poets have whitened at your high renown.
> We stand among the many millions who

Do hourly wait to pass your pathway down.
You, so familiar, once were strange: we tried
To live as of your presence unaware.
But now in every road on every side
We see your straight and steadfast signpost there.

I think it like that signpost in my land,
Hoary and tall, which pointed me to go
Upward, into the hills, on the right hand,
Where the mists swim and the winds shriek and blow,
A homeless land and friendless, but a land
I did not know and that I wished to know.

It is significant that Sorley first entitled this poem
'Death on the Downs', for in it he recaptures something
of the mystery, fear and excitement of being on the
Marlborough downs in the mist, which in turn reflects
his ambivalent attitude towards death. For he both fears
and welcomes an event which may lead to the heart of
the mystery of existence. The signpost itself is based on
an actual signpost on the Marlborough downs, which he
had possibly been tempted but afraid to follow 'Upwards,
into the hills'. Though he seems to imply a belief in an
after-life, there is no suggestion of a Christian interpret-
ation of death, as an entry to Heaven or Hell, but a more
elemental belief that it is a journey—Shakespeare's 'un-
discover'd country from whose bourn no traveller re-
turns'.

In his second sonnet Sorley develops the idea of the
familiarity of Death in wartime and the attraction of a
chance to start again, with a 'slate rubbed clean'. By
using such an ordinary domestic metaphor as a bucket

he tries to avoid romanticizing death as he feels Rupert Brooke has done, though in the last three lines he does not hesitate to point out the true pathos and glory of an early death:

Such, such is Death: no triumph: no defeat:
Only an empty pail, a slate rubbed clean,
A merciful putting away of what has been.

And this we know: Death is not Life effete,
Life crushed, the broken pail. We who have seen
So marvellous things know well the end not yet.

Victor and vanquished are a-one in death:
Coward and brave: friend, foe. Ghosts do not say
'Come, what was your record when you drew breath?'
But a big blot has hid each yesterday
So poor, so manifestly incomplete.
And your bright Promise, withered long and sped,
Is touched, stirs, rises, opens and grows sweet
And blossoms and is you, when you are dead.

The sonnet form has here been given an unusual turn by its division into two short stanzas of three lines each and a long concluding octet, with the three parts linked by an intricate rhyme scheme which includes half-rhyme. The abrupt opening monosyllables suggest a direct approach to the subject borne out by the use of the word 'Death', rather than a euphemism. Contrast is used throughout to suggest first that death cannot be defined by easy extremes—'no triumph: no defeat'; then that death is a leveller, making all men equal—'Victor and vanquished . . . coward and brave: friend, foe'—and that even war becomes insignificant in the face of death. The poem can be read as Sorley's attempt to formulate a philosophy of living which will help him to face the daily possibility of dying. On the Western Front he is learning, as Unamuno put it, to 'live in the thought of death'.

Of the six poems specifically concerned with war, four are sonnets. As I suggested earlier, Sorley probably chose this disciplined form in order to gain the greatest control possible over his highly emotive subject matter. This is best illustrated by his last sonnet, 'When You See Millions of the Mouthless Dead', which is to my mind his finest poem. The sonnet opens with a striking image, reminiscent of the disintegrating faces of Goya's 'black' paintings and the silent horror of the scene is brought out through the repetition of soft *m*s, *l*s and *s*s contrasted with harsh *d*s.

> When you see millions of the mouthless dead
> Across your dreams in pale battalions go.

'Mouthless' here also implies an inability to speak and this is backed up by 'deaf' and 'blind' later on, thus emphasizing the impossibility of communicating with the dead. The resulting sense of negation is further emphasized by a long list of actual negatives: 'Say not . . . need not . . . Give them not . . . It is not . . . Nor tears . . . Nor honour . . . None wears . . .' Thus the main body of the poem is shaped quite naturally round a series of negative commands, which are clearly meant to counteract Rupert Brooke's famous 'Think only this of me':

Say not soft things as other men have said,
That you'll remember. For you need not so.
Give them not praise. For, deaf, how should they know
It is not curses heaped on each gashed head?
Nor tears. Their blind eyes see not your tears flow.
Nor honour. It is easy to be dead.

The potentially emotive material is offset by strictly controlled syntactical patterns based on the repetition of various negatives. In sharp contrast to these negatives is the positive command of the opening line of the sestet, 'Say only this,' which leads us to expect something more hopeful and perhaps closer to Brooke. However, all that the poet will concede is a bleak statement of fact and an even bleaker echo from the *Iliad* to remind us that the dead are not necessarily very noble: 'Say only this, "They are dead." Then add thereto, "Yet many a better one has died before."' The use of direct speech at this point emphasizes the importance of this recognition and in the last four lines Sorley hammers home the unromantic truth he has been forced to accept about death:

Then, scanning all the o'ercrowded mass, should you
Perceive one face that you loved heretofore,
It is a spook. None wears the face you knew.
Great death has made all his for evermore.

The last line is more rhetorical than the rest and slightly at odds with the rather colloquial 'spook' of the line before, but it is in keeping with the gravity of the message. Sorley's personification of the power of death brings to mind the Apocalyptic Visions of Revelations.

It is, admittedly, a flourish, but not one that contradicts the views that precede it, since it emphasizes the levelling process of death. Apart from a few unfortunate archaisms, such as 'heretofore', which would almost certainly have been ironed out in revision, the diction is simple, in keeping with the stark simplicity of the message. The imagery is also fairly straightforward; the use of 'gashed head' and 'pale battalions' reminds us that Sorley is writing his poem in the midst of actual fighting. (The poem was found in his kit after his death.) His restraint in not giving more gruesome physical details nor making more direct references to the subject of his piece, adds to the dreamlike quality he obviously wishes to convey. At the same time it makes us even more aware of the nightmarish existence he was living in the last few days of his life when even the little sleep he could snatch was invaded by corpses. The use of the word 'spook' in the penultimate line reinforces the sense he gives of being haunted.

There can be no doubt that Sorley had seen through the romantic myth of war, but we can only conjecture what he would have gone on to. He had already rejected the realism Sassoon and Owen were to develop so skilfully and he had only a small share of Rosenberg's vision of the grotesque. There is certainly nothing in the three years' fighting which followed his death to suggest that he would have felt very differently about war had he survived. John Masefield, who believed that Sorley was potentially the greatest poet lost in the war, predicted that he might have become our greatest dramatist since Shakespeare. Yet there is little evidence to support this claim. Sorley attempted drama only once in 'The Other

Wise Man', which is in no way outstanding. Admittedly he had the detachment necessary to the great dramatist and was increasingly attracted to Shakespeare and Goethe. Possibly he could have written something akin to Hardy's *The Dynasts* which he greatly admired.

A more fruitful speculation concerns his prose, in particular his letters. There are times when he seems happier in this medium than poetry, perhaps because it conveys a more rounded picture of his engaging personality. His wit and his ability to tell a good story, often against himself, are not as evident in his poetry as in his prose, though the same lucid intelligence emerges in both. There are passages in his later letters which rise to the heights of poetry, yet have all the expansiveness and detail that prose allows. Sorley undoubtedly had great talent as a prose writer, which developed rapidly in the trenches, where it was probably easier to concentrate on than poetry. It may be that he would have taken it up seriously after the war.

In fact while still at Marlborough Sorley had considered the possibility of journalism as a career, though this was closely bound up with his determination to take up social work of some kind. 'I had always an idea that when you were a fair specimen of the idle rich,' he joked with his friend Hutchinson, 'and I a journalist and socialist orator campaigning against the same at street corners, you would ask me to stay occasionally and give me oysters and champagne.' Sorley's ambition was not to become a great poet, but a great reformer of the Alexander Paterson type, and he might well have given up writing altogether had he survived the war. As it was he found himself in a curiously fluid situation. In spite of all the petty restrictions of army life it seemed to him freer and more real than the academic life he had reluctantly agreed to follow. For the first time in his somewhat conventional existence, despite the fact that he now faced almost certain death, he felt liberated. And it is from the trenches that he writes his most exultant and positive letter of all to his friend Arthur Watts:

. . . but where, while riding in your Kentish lanes, are you riding twelve months hence? I am sometimes in Mexico, selling cloth: or in Russia, doing Lord knows what: in Serbia or the Balkans: in England, never. England remains the dream, the background: at once the memory and the ideal. Sorley is the Gaelic for wanderer. I have had a conventional education: Oxford would have corked it. But this has freed the spirit, glory be. Give me *The Odyssey*, and I return the New Testament to store. Physically as well as spiritually, give me the road.

Only sometimes the horrible question of bread and butter shadows the dream: it has shadowed many, I should think. It must be tackled. But I always seek to avoid the awkward, by postponing it.

You figure in these dreams as the pioneer-sergeant. Perhaps *you* are the Odysseus, I am but one of the dog-like ἑταῖροι[1] . . . But however that may be, our lives will be πολύπλαγκτοι[2], though our paths may be different. And we will be buried by the sea —

[1] Comrades.
[2] Far-roaming.

Timon will make his everlasting mansion
Upon the beachéd verge of a salt flood,
Which twice a day with his embosséd froth
The turbulent surge shall cover.*

Details can wait—perhaps for ever.

Jean Moorcroft Wilson

*Timon of Athens, act V, scene 2—slightly altered.

34

Preface

Charles Sorley's poems were first published in book form by Cambridge University Press in January 1916, only four months after his death, under the title *Marlborough and Other Poems*. Such was their popularity that another edition, to which one more poem was added, followed in February 1916. This second edition was reprinted later the same month, again in April and yet again in May 1916. A third edition, with selections from his letters, followed in November 1916. When a fourth edition was called for in 1919 Professor Sorley, who had edited his son's poems, took the opportunity of rearranging them in a form which was 'intended to be definitive'. He also added detailed notes to this fourth edition and one of his son's translations from Horace. The fifth edition, in 1922, and the sixth, in the publishers' 'Miscellany series', in 1932 followed the text of the fourth edition, apart from one or two minor alterations made from manuscripts.

Since the manuscripts of only thirteen of Sorley's poems have survived,* I have followed Professor Sorley's

*The following manuscripts were sent to the Master of Marlborough College in June 1949 where they are now preserved: 'Barbury Camp'; 'East Kennet Church at Evening'; 'Autumn Dawn'; 'Return'; 'Richard Jefferies'; 'Marlborough'; 'Two Sonnets'; 'In Memoriam, S.C.W., V.C.'; 'Verses for C1 House Concert'; 'Expectans Expectavi' and 'It was Spring'. The MS. of 'I Have not Brought My Odyssey' is owned by John Bain's son, Joseph Bain. The editor would be interested to learn of the whereabouts of any other Sorley MSS.

readings, except where these differ from the manuscripts, notably in the case of 'I have not brought my Odyssey'. I have drawn on Professor Sorley's notes, which appear here in amended form. I have not, however, followed his arrangement exactly. Though I like Professor Sorley's attempt to divide his son's poems into four categories ('Of the Downs', 'Of School', 'Of Life and Thought' and 'Of War and Death'), this creates certain awkwardnesses of chronology. Whilst preserving and at times restoring chronology, I have now placed his first apprentice poems and one or two occasional verses at the end, since they do not seem to me a good introduction to Sorley. (They are, nevertheless, invaluable to an understanding of his development and his personality.)

I have also added a number of poems not included in any previous edition.

It remains only for me to remind readers that most of Sorley's later and best work was written under difficult conditions in wartime England and France. In fact Sorley himself rejected the idea of publication in his lifetime because he felt the lack of revision keenly. There is no doubt that had he lived he would have remedied this. The wonder is that his war poems are as skilful as they are.

J.M.W.

The Poems

I

Barbury Camp

We burrowed night and day with tools of lead,
Heaped the bank up and cast it in a ring
And hurled the earth above. And Caesar said,
'Why, it is excellent. I like the thing.'
We, who are dead,
Made it, and wrought, and Caesar liked the thing.

And here we strove, and here we felt each vein
Ice-bound, each limb fast-frozen, all night long.
And here we held communion with the rain
That lashed us into manhood with its thong,
Cleansing through pain.
And the wind visited us and made us strong.

Up from around us, numbers without name,
Strong men and naked, vast, on either hand
Pressing us in, they came. And the wind came
And bitter rain, turning grey all the land.
That was our game,
To fight with men and storms, and it was grand.

For many days we fought them, and our sweat
Watered the grass, making it spring up green,
Blooming for us. And, if the wind was wet,
Our blood wetted the wind, making it keen
With the hatred
And wrath and courage that our blood had been.

So, fighting men and winds and tempests, hot
With joy and hate and battle-lust, we fell
Where we fought. And God said, 'Killed at last
    then? What!
Ye that are too strong for heaven, too clean for hell,
(God said) stir not.
This be your heaven, or, if ye will, your hell.'

So again we fight and wrestle, and again
Hurl the earth up and cast it in a ring.
But when the wind comes up, driving the rain
(Each rain-drop a fiery steed), and the mists rolling
Up from the plain,
This wild procession, this impetuous thing,

Hold us amazed. We mount the wind-cars, then
Whip up the steeds and drive through all the world,
Searching to find somewhere some brethren,
Sons of the winds and waters of the world.
We, who were men,
Have sought, and found no men in all this world.

Wind, that has blown here always ceaselessly,
Bringing, if any man can understand,
Might to the mighty, freedom to the free;
Wind, that has caught us, cleansed us, made us grand,
Wind that is we
(We that were men)—make men in all this land,

That so may live and wrestle and hate, that when
They fall at last exultant, as we fell,
And come to God, God may say 'Do you come then

Mildly enquiring, is it heaven or hell?
Why! Ye were men!
Back to your winds and rains. Be these your heaven
    and hell!'

24 March 1913

First published in *Marlborough and Other Poems*, January 1916.
Barbury Camp is on the northern escarpment of the
Marlborough downs, between five and six miles north
by west from Marlborough. The camp on the summit is
of pre-Roman origin. The preference for rain and windy
weather, shown in this and other poems in the book, has
suggested the poem entitled 'Sorley's Weather' by Robert
Graves (*Fairies and Fusiliers*, 1917) which ends with the
verse,

    Yet rest there, Shelley, on the sill,
        For though the winds come frorely
    I'm away to the rain-blown hill
        And the ghost of Sorley.

2
Rooks

There, where the rusty iron lies,
  The rooks are cawing all the day.
Perhaps no man, until he dies,
  Will understand them, what they say.

The evening makes the sky like clay.
  The slow wind waits for night to rise.
The world is half-content. But they

Still trouble all the trees with cries,
  That know, and cannot put away,
The yearning to the soul that flies
  From day to night, from night to day.

21 June 1913

First published in *The Marlburian*, 10 July 1913.
The rookery referred to is evidently that in what Marlburians called the Wilderness which was between C House
and the bathing-place, and was visible from Sorley's
dormitory window. Underneath the trees in the Wilderness a good deal of rubbish (rusty iron, etc.) had been
thrown.

3
Rooks II

There is such cry in all these birds,
  More than can ever be express'd;
If I should put it into words,
  You would agree it were not best
  To wake such wonder from its rest.

But since to-night the world is still
  And only they and I astir,
We are united, will to will,
  By bondage tighter, tenderer
  Than any lovers ever were.

And if, of too much labouring,
  All that I see around should die
(There is such sleep in each green thing,
  Such weariness in all the sky),
  We would live on, these birds and I.

Yet how? since everything must pass
  At evening with the sinking sun,
And Christ is gone, and Barabbas,
  Judas and Jesus, gone, clean gone,
  Then how shall I live on?

Yet surely Judas must have heard
  Amidst his torments the long cry
Of some lone Israelitish bird,
  And on it, ere he came to die,
  Thrown all his spirit's agony.

43

And that immortal cry which welled
   For Judas, ever afterwards
Passion on passion still has swelled
   And sweetened: so to-night these birds
   Will take my words, will take my words,

And wrapping them in music meet
   Will sing their spirit through the sky,
Strange and unsatisfied and sweet:
   That, when stock-dead am I, am I,
   O, that can never die!

25 July 1913

First published in *The Marlburian*, 28 July 1913.

4
Stones

This field is almost white with stones
    That cumber all its thirsty crust.
And underneath, I know, are bones,
    And all around is death and dust.

And if you love a livelier hue —
    O, if you love the youth of year,
When all is clean and green and new,
    Depart. There is no summer here.

Albeit, to me there lingers yet
    In this forbidding stony dress
The impotent and dim regret
    For some forgotten restlessness.

Dumb, imperceptibly astir,
    These relics of an ancient race,
These men, in whom the dead bones were
    Still fortifying their resting-place.

Their field of life was white with stones;
    Good fruit to earth they never brought.
O, in these bleached and buried bones
    Was neither love nor faith nor thought.

But like the wind in this bleak place,
    Bitter and bleak and sharp they grew,
And bitterly they ran their race,
    A brutal, bad, unkindly crew:

Souls like the dry earth, hearts like stone,
Brains like that barren bramble-tree:
Stern, sterile, senseless, mute, unknown —
But bold, O, bolder far than we!

14 July 1913

First published in *The Marlburian*, 28 July 1913.
In this case, and in a few other cases, the text in the book varies slightly from that given in *The Marlburian*. In these variations the author's manuscript has been followed.

5
East Kennet Church at Evening

I stood amongst the corn, and watched
    The evening coming down.
The rising vale was like a queen,
    And the dim church her crown.

Crown-like it stood against the hills.
    Its form was passing fair.
I almost saw the tribes go up
    To offer incense there.

And far below the long vale stretched.
    As a sleeper she did seem
That after some brief restlessness
    Has now begun to dream.

(All day the wakefulness of men,
    Their lives and labours brief,
Have broken her long troubled sleep.
    Now, evening brings relief.)

There was no motion there nor sound.
    She did not seem to rise.
Yet was she wrapping herself in
    Her grey of night-disguise.

For now no church nor tree nor fold
    Was visible to me:
Only that fading into one
    Which God must sometimes see.

No coloured glory streaked the sky
    To mark the sinking sun.
There was no redress in the west
    To tell that day was done.

Only, the greyness of the eve
    Grew fuller than before.
And, in its fulness, it made one
    Of what had once been more.

There was much beauty in that sight
    That man must not long see.
God dropped the kindly veil of night
    Between its end and me.

24 July 1913

First published in *The Marlburian*, 3 December 1913.
East Kennet is a village on the Kennet between four and
five miles west of Marlborough. A correspondent familiar
with the district, thought that the church seen by the
author from the cornfield was not that of East Kennet
but the neighbouring church of West Overton.

6
Autumn Dawn

And this is morning. Would you think
That this was the morning, when the land
Is full of heavy eyes that blink
Half-opened, and the tall trees stand
Too tired to shake away the drops
Of passing night that cling around
Their branches and weigh down their tops:
And the grey sky leans on the ground?
The thrush sings once or twice, but stops
Affrighted by the silent sound.
The sheep, scarce moving, munches, moans.
The slow herd mumbles, thick with phlegm.
The grey road-mender, hacking stones,
Is now become as one of them.

Old mother Earth has rubbed her eyes
And stayed, so senseless, lying down.
Old mother is too tired to rise
And lay aside her grey nightgown,
And come with singing and with strength
In loud exuberance of day,
Swift-darting. She is tired at length,
Done up, past bearing, you would say.
She'll come no more in lust of strife,
In hedge's leap, and wild bird's cries,
In winds that cut you like a knife,
In days of laughter and swift skies,
That palpably pulsate with life,

With life that kills, with life that dies.
But in a morning such as this
Is neither life nor death to see,
Only that state which some call bliss,
Grey, hopeless, immortality.

Earth is at length bedrid. She is
Supinest of the things that be:
And stilly, heavy with long years,
Brings forth such days in dumb regret,
Immortal days, that rise in tears,
And cannot, though they strive to, set.

* * *

The mists do move. The wind takes breath.
The sun appeareth over there,
And with red fingers hasteneth
From Earth's grey bed the clothes to tear,
And strike the heavy mist's dank tent.
And Earth uprises with a sigh.
She is astir. She is not spent.
And yet she lives and yet can die.
The grey road-mender from the ditch
Looks up. He has not looked before.
The stunted tree sways like the witch
It was: 'tis living witch once more.
The winds are washen. In the deep
Dew of the morn they've washed. The skies
Are changing dress. The clumsy sheep
Bound, and earth's many bosoms rise,
And earth's green tresses spring and leap
About her brow. The earth has eyes,

The earth has voice, the earth has breath,
As o'er the land and through the air,
With wingéd sandals, Life and Death
Speed hand in hand—that winsome pair!

16 September 1913

First published in *The Marlburian*, 9 October 1913.
This poem, said the author, in sending a copy of it home
from Germany, 'has too much copy from Meredith in it,
but I value it as being (with 'Return') a memorial of my
walk to Marlborough last September' (1913). The scenery of this walk is recalled in parts of 'I have not brought
my Odyssey'.

7
Return

Still stand the downs so wise and wide?
　　Still shake the trees their tresses grey?
I thought their beauty might have died
　　Since I had been away.

I might have known the things I love,
　　The winds, the flocking birds' full cry,
The trees that toss, the downs that move,
　　Were longer things than I.

Lo, Earth that bows before the wind,
　　With wild green children overgrown,
And all her bosoms, many-whinned,
　　Receive me as their own.

The birds are hushed and fled: the cows
　　Have ceased at last to make long moan.
They only think to browse and browse
　　Until the night is grown.

The wind is stiller than it was,
　　And dumbness holds the closing day.
The earth says not a word, because
　　It has no word to say.

The dear soft grasses under foot
Are silent to the listening ear.
Yet beauty never can be mute,
And some will always hear.

18 September 1913

First published in *Marlborough and Other Poems*, January 1916.
This poem, like 'Autumn Dawn', sprang from Sorley's walk to Marlborough in September 1913.
Line 11, *many-whinned*: covered with gorse or furze ('whin'=gorse/furze).

8
Richard Jefferies
(Liddington Castle)

I see the vision of the vale
   Rise teeming to the rampart down,
The fields and, far below, the pale
   Red-roofédness of Swindon town.

But though I see all things remote,
   I cannot see them with the eyes
With which ere now the man from Coate
   Looked down and wondered and was wise.

He knew the healing balm of night,
   The strong and sweeping joy of day,
The sensible and dear delight
   Of life, the pity of decay.

And many wondrous words he wrote,
   And something good to man he showed,
About the entering in of Coate,
   There, on the dusty Swindon road.

19 September 1913

First published in *The Marlburian*, 9 October 1913.
This poem is a result of the same walk as 'Autumn Dawn'
and 'Return'. Liddington Castle is about seven miles
north by east from Marlborough and, like Barbury Camp,
guards the northern frontier of the downs. Describing a

walk three months before, Sorley wrote, 'I then scaled Liddington Castle, which is no more a castle than I am, but a big hill with a fine Roman camp on the top, and a view all down the Vale of the White Horse to the north and the Kennet valley to the south. I sat there for about an hour, reading *Wild Life in a Southern County*, with which I had come armed—the most appropriate place in the world to read it from, as it was on Liddington Castle that Richard Jefferies wrote it and many others of his books, and as it is Jefferies' description of how he saw the country from there.'

Line 7, *Coate*: a village to'the south (now a suburb) of Swindon, and the birthplace of Jefferies (1848-1887).

9
The Other Wise Man

(SCENE: *A valley with a wood on one side and a road run-ning up to a distant hill: as it might be, the valley to the east of West Woods, that runs up to Oare Hill, only much larger.* TIME: *Autumn. Four wise men are marching hillward along the road.*)

ONE WISE MAN

I wonder where the valley ends?
On, comrades, on.

ANOTHER WISE MAN

The rain-red road,
Still shining sinuously, bends
Leagues upwards.

A THIRD WISE MAN

To the hill, O friends,
To seek the star that once has glowed
Before us; turning not to right
Nor left, nor backward once looking.
Till we have clomb — and with the night
We see the King.

ALL THE WISE MEN

The King! The King!

THE THIRD WISE MAN

Long is the road but—

A FOURTH WISE MAN

Brother, see,
There, to the left, a very aisle
Composed of every sort of tree—

THE FIRST WISE MAN

Still onward—

THE FOURTH WISE MAN

Oak and beech and birch,
Like a church, but homelier than church,
The black trunks for its walls of tile;
Its roof, old leaves; its floor, beech nuts;
The squirrels its congregation—

THE SECOND WISE MAN

Tuts!
For still we journey—

THE FOURTH WISE MAN

But the sun weaves
A water-web across the grass,
Binding their tops. You must not pass
The water cobweb.

THE THIRD WISE MAN

Hush! I say.
Onward and upward till the day—

THE FOURTH WISE MAN

Brother, that tree has crimson leaves.
You'll never see its like again.
Don't miss it. Look, it's bright with rain—

THE FIRST WISE MAN

O prating tongue. On, on.

THE FOURTH WISE MAN

And there
A toad-stool, nay, a goblin stool.
No toad sat on a thing so fair.
Wait, while I pluck—and there's—and here's
A whole ring . . . what? . . . berries?

(*The Fourth Wise Man drops behind, botanizing.*)

THE WISEST OF THE REMAINING THREE
WISE MEN

O fool!
Fool, fallen in this vale of tears.
His hand had touched the plough: his eyes
Looked back: no more with us, his peers,

58

He'll climb the hill and front the skies
And see the Star, the King, the Prize.
But we, the seekers, we who see
Beyond the mists of transiency —
Our feet down in the valley still
Are set, our eyes are on the hill.
Last night the star of God has shone,
And so we journey, up and on,
With courage clad, with swiftness shod,
All thoughts of earth behind us cast,
Until we see the lights of God,
— And what will be the crown at last?

ALL THREE WISE MEN

On, on.

(*They pass on: it is already evening when the Other Wise Man limps along the road, still botanizing.*)

THE OTHER WISE MAN

A vale of tears, they said!
A valley made of woes and fears,
To be passed by with muffled head
Quickly. I have not seen the tears,
Unless they take the rain for tears,
And certainly the place is wet.
Rain-laden leaves are ever licking
Your cheeks and hands . . . I can't get on.
There's a toad-stool that wants picking.

59

There, just there, a little up,
What strange things to look upon
With pink hood and orange cup!
And there are acorns, yellow—green . . .
They said the King was at the end.
They must have been
Wrong. For here, here, I intend
To search for him, for surely here
Are all the wares of the old year,
And all the beauty and bright prize,
And all God's colours meetly showed,
Green for the grass, blue for the skies,
Red for the rain upon the road;
And anything you like for trees,
But chiefly yellow, brown and gold,
Because the year is growing old
And loves to paint her children these.
I tried to follow . . . but, what do you think?
The mushrooms here are pink!
And there's old clover with black polls,
Black-headed clover, black as coals,
And toad-stools, sleek as ink!
And there are such heaps of little turns
Off the road, wet with old rain:
Each little vegetable lane
Of moss and old decaying ferns,
Beautiful in decay,
Snatching a beauty from whatever may
Be their lot, dark-red and luscious: till there pass'd
Over the many-coloured earth a grey
Film. It was evening coming down at last.
And all things hid their faces, covering up

Their peak or hood or bonnet or bright cup
In greyness, and the beauty faded fast,
With all the many-coloured coat of day.
Then I looked up, and lo! the sunset sky
Had taken the beauty from the autumn earth.
Such colour, O such colour, could not die.
The trees stood black against such revelry
Of lemon-gold and purple and crimson dye.
And even as the trees, so I
Stood still and worshipped, though by evening's birth
I should have capped the hills and seen the King.
The King? The King?
I must be miles away from my journey's end;
The others must be now nearing
The summit, glad. By now they wend
Their way far, far, ahead, no doubt.
I wonder if they've reached the end.
If they have, I have not heard them shout.

1 December 1913

First published in *The Marlburian*, 10 February 1914.
This poem marks Sorley's rejection of orthodox religion.
Oare Hill is on the north-eastern border of Pewsey Vale
between three and four miles from Marlborough College.
West Woods are on the western side of the valley and
nearer Marlborough.

10

Marlborough

Crouched where the open upland billows down
   Into the valley where the river flows,
She is as any other country town,
   That little lives or marks or hears or knows.

And she can teach but little. She has not
   The wonder and the surging and the roar
Of striving cities. Only things forgot
   That once were beautiful, but now no more,

Has she to give us. Yet to one or two
   She first brought knowledge, and it was for her
To open first our eyes, until we knew
   How great, immeasurably great, we were.

I, who have walked along her downs in dreams,
   And known her tenderness, and felt her might,
And sometimes by her meadows and her streams
   Have drunk deep-storied secrets of delight:

Have had my moments there, when I have been
   Unwittingly aware of something more,
Some beautiful aspect, that I had seen
   With mute, unspeculative eyes before;

Have had my times, when, though the earth did wear
    Her self-same trees and grasses, I could see
The revelation that is always there,
    But somehow is not always clear to me.

II

So, long ago, one halted on his way
    And sent his company and cattle on;
His caravans trooped darkling far away
    Into the night, and he was left alone.

And he was left alone. And, lo, a man
    There wrestled with him till the break of day.
The brook was silent and the night was wan.
    And when the dawn was come, he passed away.

The sinew of the hollow of his thigh
    Was shrunken, as he wrestled there alone.
The brook was silent, but the dawn was nigh.
    The stranger named him Israel and was gone.

And the sun rose on Jacob; and he knew
    That he was no more Jacob, but had grown
A more immortal, vaster spirit, who
    Had seen God face to face, and still lived on.

The plain that seemed to stretch away to God,
    The brook that saw and heard and knew no fear,
Were now the self-same soul as he who stood
    And waited for his brother to draw near.

63

For God had wrestled with him, and was gone.
　　He looked around, and only God remained.
The dawn, the desert, he and God were one.
　　— And Esau came to meet him, travel-stained.

III

So, there, when sunset made the downs look new
　　And earth gave up her colours to the sky,
And far away the little city grew
　　Half into sight, new-visioned was my eye.

I, who have lived, and trod her lovely earth,
　　Raced with her winds and listened to her birds,
Have cared but little for their worldly worth
　　Nor sought to put my passion into words.

But now it's different; and I have no rest
　　Because my hand must search, dissect and spell
The beauty that is better not expressed,
　　The thing that all can feel, but none can tell.

1 March 1914

First published as the title poem in *Marlborough and
Other Poems* in January 1916.
The origin of the story in 'II' is to be found in Genesis
32.23-33.1.

The Song of the Ungirt Runners

We swing ungirded hips,
And lightened are our eyes,
The rain is on our lips,
We do not run for prize.
We know not whom we trust
Nor whitherward we fare,
But we run because we must
    Through the great wide air.

The waters of the seas
Are troubled as by storm.
The tempest strips the trees
And does not leave them warm.
Does the tearing tempest pause?
Do the tree-tops ask it why?
So we run without a cause
    'Neath the big bare sky.

The rain is on our lips,
We do not run for prize.
But the storm the water whips
And the wave howls to the skies.
The winds arise and strike it
And scatter it like sand,
And we run because we like it
    Through the broad bright land.

First published in *Marlborough and Other Poems* in January 1916. The poem is undated, but it was received by Sorley's parents in December 1914, while Sorley was training in England.

12

German Rain

The heat came down and sapped away my powers.
The laden heat came down and drowsed my brain,
Till through the weight of overcoming hours
        I felt the rain.

Then suddenly I saw what more to see
I never thought: old things renewed, retrieved.
The rain that fell in England fell on me,
        And I believed.

First published in *Marlborough and Other Poems* in January 1916. The poem is undated, but was obviously written while Sorley was at Jena in the summer of 1914.

13
'All the hills and vales along'

All the hills and vales along
Earth is bursting into song,
And the singers are the chaps
Who are going to die perhaps.
 O sing, marching men,
 Till the valleys ring again.
 Give your gladness to earth's keeping,
 So be glad, when you are sleeping.

Cast away regret and rue,
Think what you are marching to.
Little live, great pass.
Jesus Christ and Barabbas
Were found the same day.
This died, that went his way.
 So sing with joyful breath.
 For why, you are going to death.
 Teeming earth will surely store
 All the gladness that you pour.

Earth that never doubts nor fears,
Earth that knows of death, not tears,
Earth that bore with joyful ease
Hemlock for Socrates,
Earth that blossomed and was glad
'Neath the cross that Christ had,
Shall rejoice and blossom too
When the bullet reaches you.

Wherefore, men marching
On the road to death, sing!
Pour your gladness on earth's head,
So be merry so be dead.

From the hills and valleys earth
Shouts back the sound of mirth,
Tramp of feet and lilt of song
Ringing all the road along
All the music of their going,
Ringing swinging glad song-throwing,
Earth will echo still, when foot
Lies numb and voice mute.
On marching men, on
To the gates of death with song.
Sow your gladness for earth's reaping,
So you may be glad, though sleeping.
Strew your gladness on earth's bed,
So be merry, so be dead.

First published in *Marlborough and Other Poems* in January 1916.
Professor Sorley says that there is external evidence, though it is not quite conclusive, for dating this poem in August 1914. It was not sent home until April 1915, however.

14
To Germany

You are blind like us. Your hurt no man designed,
And no man claimed the conquest of your land.
But gropers both through fields of thought confined
We stumble and we do not understand.
You only saw your future bigly planned,
And we, the tapering paths of our own mind,
And in each other's dearest ways we stand,
And hiss and hate. And the blind fight the blind.

When it is peace, then we may view again
With new-won eyes each other's truer form
And wonder. Grown more loving-kind and warm
We'll grasp firm hands and laugh at the old pain,
When it is peace. But until peace, the storm
The darkness and the thunder and the rain.

First published in *Marlborough and Other Poems* in January 1916.
Professor Sorley claims that there is the same evidence for dating this poem in August 1914 as for 'All the Hills and Vales'. It too was not sent home until April 1915.

15
To Poets

We are the homeless, even as you,
Who hope and never can begin.
Our hearts are wounded through and through
Like yours, but our hearts bleed within.
We too make music, but our tones
'Scape not the barrier of our bones.

We have no comeliness like you.
We toil, unlovely, and we spin.
We start, return: we wind, undo:
We hope, we err, we strive, we sin,
We love: your love's not greater, but
The lips of our love's might stay shut.

We have the evil spirits too
That shake our soul with battle-din.
But we have an eviller spirit than you,
We have a dumb spirit within:
The exceeding bitter agony
But not the exceeding bitter cry.

September 1914

First published in *Marlborough and Other Poems* in January 1916.

16
Whom Therefore We Ignorantly Worship

These things are silent. Though it may be told
Of luminous deeds that lighten land and sea,
Strong sounding actions with broad minstrelsy
Of praise, strange hazards and adventures bold,
We hold to the old things that grow not old:
Blind, patient, hungry, hopeless (without fee
Of all our hunger and unhope are we),
To the first ultimate instinct, to God we hold.

They flicker, glitter, flicker. But we bide,
We, the blind weavers of an intense fate,
Asking but this—that we may be denied:
Desiring only desire insatiate,
Unheard, unnamed, unnoticed, crucified
To our unutterable faith, we wait.

September 1914

First published in *Marlborough and Other Poems* in January 1916.
The title echoes The Acts of the Apostles, 17, 23: 'Whom therefore ye ignorantly worship, him declare I unto you'.
   This poem had its origin in Sorley's journey from the Officers' Training Camp at Churn in Berkshire to join his regiment at Shorncliffe on 18 September 1914, when he arrived at Paddington Station shortly before the special train left which took the Marlborough boys back

A hundred thousand million mites we sway
Writing and tossing on the eternal plain,
Some black with death—but most are bright with Day!
Who sent us forth? Who brings us home again?

September 1914

First published in *Marlborough and Other Poems* in January 1916.

18
Lost

Across my past imaginings
   Has dropped a blindness silent and slow.
My eye is bent on other things
   Than those it once did see and know.

I may not think on those dear lands
   (O far away and long ago!)
Where the old battered signpost stands
   And silently the four roads go

East, west, south and north,
   And the cold winter winds do blow.
And what the evening will bring forth
   Is not for me nor you to know.

December 1914

First published in *Marlborough and Other Poems* in January 1916.
This poem was sent to Sorley's friend, A.E. Hutchinson, in December 1914. Sorley wrote, 'I have tried for long to express in words the impression that the land north of Marlborough must leave. . . . Simplicity, paucity of words, monotony almost, and mystery are necessary. I think I have got it at last.' Sending it home, along with a number of others, in April 1915, he described it as 'the last of my Marlborough poems.'

Line 7: the *signpost*, which figures here as well as else-where in the poems, stood at 'the junction of the grass tracks on the Aldbourne [Poulton] downs—to Ogbourne, Marlborough, Mildenhall, and Aldbourne. It stands up quite alone.' Sorley's signpost has recently been replaced by a new one.

19

Brand

Thou trod'st the shifting sand path where man's race is.
The print of thy soft sandals is still clear.
I too have trodden it those prints a-near,
But the sea washes out my tired foot-traces.
And all that thou hast healed and holpen here
I yearned to heal and help and wipe the tear
Away. But still I trod unpeopled spaces.
I had no twelve to follow my pure paces.
For I had thy misgivings and thy fear,
Thy crown of scorn, thy suffering's sharp spear,
Thy hopes, thy longings — only not thy dear
Love (for my crying love would no man hear),
Thy will to love, but not thy love's sweet graces,
That deep firm foothold which no sea erases.
I think that thou wast I in bygone places
In an intense eliminated year.
Now born again in days that are more drear
I wander unfulfilled: and see strange faces.

First published in *Marlborough and Other Poems*, January
1916.
'Brand' and the following poem, 'Peer Gynt' were entitled
'Two Songs from Ibsen's Dramatic Poems' in Sorley's
manuscript. They are not translations from Ibsen, but
Sorley's own impressions of the dramatist's characters.
They are both undated, but Sorley sent them home to
his parents in April 1915, which suggests that they were

written earlier that year. They may have been planned and even written during Sorley's stay in Germany, when he was seeing Ibsen performed and rereading his works in German.

20
Peer Gynt

When we was young and beautiful and bold
We hated him, for he was very strong.
But when he came back home again, quite old,
And wounded too, we could not hate him long.

For kingliness and conquest pranced he forth
Like some high-stepping charger bright with foam.
And south he strode and east and west and north
With need of crowns and never need of home.

Enraged we heard high tidings of his strength
And cursed his long forgetfulness. We swore
That should he come back home some eve at length,
We would deny him, we would bar the door!

And then he came. The sound of those tired feet!
And all our home and all our hearts are his,
Where bitterness, grown weary, turns to sweet,
And envy, purged by longing, pity is.

And pillows rest beneath the withering cheek,
And hands are laid the battered brows above,
And he whom we had hated, waxen weak,
First in his weakness learns a little love.

First published in *Marlborough and Other Poems*, January
1916. See note to 'Brand', pages 78-79.

21

'If I have suffered pain'

If I have suffered pain
It is because I would.
I willed it. 'Tis no good
To murmur or complain.
I have not served the law
That keeps the earth so fair
And gives her clothes to wear,
Raiment of joy and awe.

For all, that bow to bless
That law, shall sure abide.
But man shall not abide,
And hence his gloriousness.
Lo, evening earth doth lie
All-beauteous and all peace.
Man only does not cease
From striving and from cry.

Sun sets in peace: and soon
The moon will shower her peace.
O law-abiding moon,
You hold your peace in fee!
Man, leastways, will not be
Down-bounden to these laws.
Man's spirit sees no cause
To serve such laws as these.

There yet are many seas
For man to wander in.
He yet must find out sin,
If aught of pleasance there
Remain for him to store,
His rovings to increase,
In quest of many a shore
Forbidden still to fare.

Peace sleeps the earth upon,
And sweet peace on the hill.
The waves that whimper still
At their long law-serving
(O flowing sad complaint!)
Come on and are back drawn.
Man only owns no king,
Man only is not faint.

You see, the earth is bound.
You see, the man is free.
For glorious liberty
He suffers and would die.
Grudge not then suffering
Or chastisemental cry.
O let his pain abound,
Earth's truant and earth's king!

First published in *Marlborough and Other Poems*, January 1916.
This poem is undated, but Sorley sent it home to his parents in April 1915.

22
Deus Loquitur

That's what I am: a thing of no desire,
With no path to discover and no plea
To offer up, so be my altar fire
May burn before the hearth continuously,
To be
For wayward men a steadfast light to see.

They know me in the morning of their days,
But ere noontide forsake me, to discern
New lore and hear new riddles. But moonrays
Bring them back footsore, humble, bent, a-burn
To turn
And warm them by my fire which they did spurn.

They flock together like tired birds. 'We sought
Full many stars in many skies to see,
But ever knowledge disappointment brought.
Thy light alone, Lord, burneth steadfastly.'
Ah me!
Then it is I who fain would wayward be.

First published in *Marlborough and Other Poems*, January
1916.
Title: God speaks.
The poem is undated, but Sorley sent it home to his
parents in April 1915.

23
Le Revenant

He trod the oft-remembered lane
   (Now smaller-seeming than before
   When first he left his father's door
For newer things), but still quite plain

(Though half-benighted now) upstood
   Old landmarks, ghosts across the lane
   That brought the Bygone back again:
Shorn haystacks and the rooky wood;

The guide post, too, which once he clomb
   To read the figures: fourteen miles
   To Swindon, four to Clinton Stiles,
And only half a mile to home:

And far away the one homestead, where—
   Behind the day now not quite set
   So that he saw in silhouette
Its chimneys still stand black and bare—

He noticed that the trees were not
   So big as when he journeyed last
   That way. For greatly now he passed
Striding above the hedges, hot

With hopings, as he passed by where
   A lamp before him glanced and stayed
   Across his path, so that his shade
Seemed like a giant's moving there.

The dullness of the sunken sun
    He marked not, nor how dark it grew,
    Nor that strange flapping bird that flew
Above: he thought but of the One . . . .

He topped the crest and crossed the fence,
    Noticed the garden that it grew
    As erst, noticed the hen-house too
(The kennel had been altered since).

It seemed so unchanged and so still.
    (Could it but be the past arisen
    For one short night from out of prison?)
He reached the big-bowed window-sill,

Lifted the window sash with care,
    Then, gaily throwing aside the blind,
    Shouted. It was a shock to find
That he was not remembered there.

At once he felt not all his pain,
    But murmuringly apologised,
    Turned, once more sought the undersized
Blown trees, and the long lanky lane,

Wondering and pondering on, past where
    A lamp before him glanced and stayed
    Across his path, so that his shade
Seemed like a giant's moving there.

First published in *Marlborough and Other Poems*, January

1916. The poem is undated, but it was received by Sorley's parents in April 1915, while Sorley was behind the lines in France.

Line 11: *Clinton Stiles* has not been identified and is probably imaginary.

24
Two Sonnets

Saints have adored the lofty soul of you.
Poets have whitened at your high renown.
We stand among the many millions who
Do hourly wait to pass your pathway down.
You, so familiar, once were strange: we tried
To live as of your presence unaware.
But now in every road on every side
We see your straight and steadfast signpost there.

I think it like that signpost in my land,
Hoary and tall, which pointed me to go
Upward, into the hills, on the right hand,
Where the mists swim and the winds shriek and blow,
A homeless land and friendless, but a land
I did not know and that I wished to know.

Such, such is Death: no triumph: no defeat:
Only an empty pail, a slate rubbed clean,
A merciful putting away of what has been.

And this we know: Death is not Life effete,
Life crushed, the broken pail. We who have seen
So marvellous things know well the end not yet.

Victor and vanquished are a-one in death:
Coward and brave: friend, foe. Ghosts do not say
'Come, what was your record when you drew breath?'
But a big blot has hid each yesterday
So poor, so manifestly incomplete.
And your bright Promise, withered long and sped,
Is touched, stirs, rises, opens and grows sweet
And blossoms and is you, when you are dead.

12 June 1915

Both these sonnets were first published in *Marlborough and Other Poems*, January 1916.
A copy of the first sonnet was sent by Sorley to a friend with the title 'Death—and the Downs'. The title here is taken from the copy Sorley sent home to his parents from France.

'There is such change in all those fields'

There is such change in all those fields,
Such motion rhythmic, ordered, free,
Where ever-glancing summer yields
Birth, fragrance, sunlight, immanency,
To make us view our rights of birth.
What shall we do? How shall we die?
We, captives of a roaming earth,
'Mid shades that life and light deny.
Blank summer's surfeit heaves in mist;
Dumb earth basks dewy-washed; while still
We whom Intelligence has kissed
Do make us shackles of our will.
And yet I know in each loud brain,
Round-clamped with laws and learning so,
Is madness more and lust of strain
Than earth's jerked godlings e'er can know.
The false Delilah of our brain
Has set us round the millstone going.
O lust of roving! lust of pain!
Our hair will not be long in growing.
Like blinded Samson round we go.
We hear the grindstone groan and cry.
Yet we are kings, we know, we know.
What shall we do? How shall we die?
Take but our pauper's gift of birth,
O let us from the grindstone free!
And tread the maddening gladdening earth
In strength close-braced with purity.

The earth is old; we ever new.
Our eyes should see no other sense
Than this, eternally to DO —
Our joy, our task, our recompense;
Up unexploréd mountains move,
Track tireless through great wastes afar,
Nor slumber in the arms of love,
Nor tremble on the brink of war;
Make Beauty and make Rest give place,
Mock Prudence loud — and she is gone,
Smite Satisfaction on the face
And tread the ghost of Ease upon.
Light-lipped and singing press we hard
Over old earth which now is worn,
Triumphant, buffeted and scarred,
By billows howled at, tempest-torn,
Toward blue horizons far away
(Which do not give the rest we need,
But some long strife, more than this play,
Some task that will be stern indeed) —
We ever new, we ever young,
We happy creatures of a day!
What will the gods say, seeing us strung
As nobly and as taut as they?

First published in the second edition of *Marlborough and Other Poems*, February 1916. This was the only original poem that Professor Sorley added to the thirty-seven poems contained in his first edition. It was sent by Sorley to his friend Arthur Watts in July 1915.

Juvenilia and Occasional Poems

The Tempest

The tempest is coming,
    The sky is so dark,
The bee has stopped humming
    And down flies the lark.

The clouds are all uttering
    Strange words in the sky;
They are growling and muttering
    As if they would die.

Some forked lightning passes
    And lights up the place,
The plains and the grasses,
    A glorious space.

It is like a story
    The light in the sky:
A moment of glory
    And then it will die.

The rain is beginning,
    The sky is so dark,
The bird has stopped singing
    And down flies the lark.

Sorley's sister, Jean Bickersteth, remembered that he wrote this poem when he was about ten, as a contribution to the school magazine she was helping to organise.

29
Verses for a C1 House Concert

I've just received an awkward invitation
At really most confoundedly short notice,
To make a kind of funeral oration
(And try and feel for once like what a poet is)
    Upon these gentlemen who've spent their guineas
    In buying O.M. Colours down at Vinnie's.

So Past and Present Members of C.1
It's just about high time that I begun.

First comes the bellower of Forty Years On,
That charming song we'll very soon shed tears on,
I'd say much more about it if I'd time to
Whose name I've tried, but cannot find a rhyme to,
A terrifying Trojan, gaunt and huge
That sometimes answers to the name of Scrooge
To see him chasing that old ball on Lower
And then to see him when he tries to throw her!
    A sixty cap—and quite a nut at hockey
    Who heads the ball, he loves it, as a rule;
    I think we all could answer 'Like a rock, he
    Is quite the best house-prefect in the school.'

Then the captain of Cricket,
Whose keenness must pick it,
A bowler whose taken of wickets a lot;
    And those splendid grey 'barnes', Sir,
    (As Cottley's to answer

95

I thought that I'd better to give it him hot.)
 And I could write hymns on
 That tie, blue and crimson,
Which all of us are so delighted he's got.
 Beyond all past memories
 Is his keenness on Emery's
Always coaching and bowling to good and to bad:
 I'm certain that C.1
 Will surely agree, one
And all, he's the best cricket captain we've had.

If you ask how we managed to capture the hockey cup
 I answer 'twas Philpot that brought it to pass.
Shall we get it next Lent Term?—unless we can lock it up??
 I wonder. For Philpot is leaving—alas!
 An excellent captain
 Incredibly wrapt in
The welfare of house—and he's leaving alas!
 And the loss of heartiness
 Next term when we're Billyless.
 Things will look like growing thin
 When we can no longer see
 That expansive rustic grin
 On the Captain's bed in B.   48

 Next we shed a tear upon
 The leaving of our Algernon.
 All, I think, agree with me
 Maltese Cross will hardly be
 Quite the same, since Clarke, A.D.
 's got an O.M. tie to go
 Up to 'Pember—don't you know?'

Next there comes a rare good fellow,
Great performer on the 'cello,
Mighty singer too—and says
That his name's de Sausmarez:
Whose heart is weak, or he'd have been
Just about a school 'Fifteen',
Whose heart is weak, but none the less,
It doesn't touch his heartiness.

If you ask me again what has made College corps like
   A regular army that never could yield:
Why! It's Field the Ferocious, or Walter the Warlike,
   Master Dashitt of 'A' House—our subaltern, Field.
   Swimmer and Subaltern
   Thanks for the trouble ta'en
With house-squad and swimming—fantastical Field!

   And then that entire—
   ly excellent Dyer,
With 'Forty' and Gymn Eight among other things.   73
   It's simply uncanny
   The way in which Fanny
Behaves if you put him near bars or near rings.
   His 'kish' is a billion
   Bright hues of vermillion
The captain of Classroom, of F and of Gym,
   His pull-throughs and balances
   Show us his talents, his
Wonderful strength—and we're now losing him.

   Another thing that grieves us sore
     Is the loss of Cullimore,

If you can imagine right
A monkey, clad in green and white,
Who has shot in that Ashburton
(Over which we'll draw a curtain),
Who is leaving I believe,
Whom we do not want to leave,
Sitting with a huge grin on
— Awfully sorry, Headington.

Then there's Mann the bugler: Mann the golfer
   Middle IV Form Blood with every upper:
And we're sorry that we've got to offer
   Our farewells so soon as this House-supper.

Then there is Bengough, with eye like a hawk
(And you should hear him — the way he can talk!)
If they'd allowed him to play in House-Matches
Gooch's keen palm would have held all the catches,
Gooch would have sent that velocipede rolling,
Gooch would have shown what he thought of their
   bowling!

   Then Monkland that wonder,
   Who bowls like the thunder,
And doesn't leave much of the other side there
   You were pretty hot on
   The Lower of Cotton
And 7 for 0 is a bit of a scare.
   With pleasure all noted
   That you're re-promoted
— A well-deserved hat-band on well-preserved hair!

Last of all, by no means least,
Phillips, wily, sly, old beast:
Phillips, sometimes known as 'Nag':
Phillips somewhat of a wag,
Phillips do you know we're grieving
That your well-known face is leaving?

So here's to each one of them, as I have said,
From Cattley our Captain to Sanger our Head.
From Dyer, the captain of classroom and Gym,
To Philpot of hockey and Field who can swim,
From Cullimore, Algernon Clarke and de Sausmarez,
Gooch who a golfer and Mann who a drummer is,
Monkland and Phillips and Headington too
Here's to you all at this hearty house-brew!

First published in *The Marlburian*, 29 July 1912. This is
the earliest of Sorley's Marlborough poems, if it can be
called such.
Line 6: *Vinnie's*: Vinney Head, the College outfitters in
Marlborough High Street.
Line 48: *B*: B House dormitory.
Line 52: The Maltese Cross is the crest of C.1 House.
Line 55: *Pember*: Pembroke College, Oxford.
Line 73: *Forty* refers to a 'forty' cap, the equivalent of
the second fifteen in rugby football.
Line 77: *Kish*, a kind of folding cushion in which Marl-
burians carried their school books.

30
The Massacre

A rendering, in verse, of a dream of the author's after a somewhat extravagant meal, for the details and sentiments of which he does not hold himself responsible

Now Vengeance is greater than Pity,
And Falsehood is mightier than Honour,
And Evil is fairer than Virtue,
And Cursing is sweeter than Prayer:
So plunder, dismantle the city,
And bring desolation upon her;
Nor heed what may harm nor may hurt you,
But leave not a living soul there!

And they heard his command, and obeyed it;
At night was the carnage begun,
The city was ravaged and raided,
By morning the carnage was done.
And never were any men gayer,
And never will men be so gay,
For oh! it was sweet to the slayer
To sling and to slash and to slay!

And from every house there was pouring
In torrents a deep crimson flood;
And down every street there was roaring
A wonderful river of blood.
And never a soul felt abhorrence
At this misery, murder and pain;

But the soldiers were drinking the torrents
And quaffing the blood of the slain!

But still in its dim desolation
The City lay wrapped in repose,
And sorrow and loud lamentation
From its citadel never up rose;
And no sound of wailing nor weeping
Was heard through the silence to creep,
For lo! that great City was sleeping,
And lo! it had died in its sleep.

First published in *The Marlburian*, 17 October 1912.

31
Rain

When the rain is coming down,
And all Court is still and bare,
And the leaves fall wrinkled, brown,
Through the kindly winter air,
And in tattered flannels I
'Sweat' beneath a tearful sky,
And the sky is dim and grey,
And the rain is coming down,
And I wander far away
From the little red-capped town:
There is something in the rain
That would bid me to remain:
There is something in the wind
That would whisper, 'Leave behind
All this land of time and rules,
Land of bells and early schools.
Latin, Greek and College food
Do you precious little good.
Leave them: if you would be free
Follow, follow, after me!'

When I reach 'Four Miler's' height,
And I look abroad again
On the skies of dirty white
And the drifting veil of rain,
And the bunch of scattered hedge
Dimly swaying on the edge,
And the endless stretch of downs

Clad in green and silver gowns;
There is something in their dress
Of bleak barren ugliness,
That would whisper, 'You have read
Of a land of light and glory:
But believe not what is said.
'Tis a kingdom bleak and hoary,
Where the winds and tempests call
And the rain sweeps over all.
Heed not what the preachers say
Of a good land far away.
Here's a better land and kind
And it is not far to find.'

Therefore, when we rise and sing
Of a distant land, so fine,
Where the bells for ever ring,
And the suns for ever shine:
Singing loud and singing grand,
Of a happy far-off land,
O! I smile to hear the song,
For I know that they are wrong,
That the happy land and gay
Is not very far away,
And that I can get there soon
Any rainy afternoon.

And when summer comes again,
And the downs are dimpling green,
And the air is free from rain,
And the clouds no longer seen:
Then I know that they have gone

To find a new camp further on,
Where there is no shining sun
To throw light on what is done,
Where the summer can't intrude
On the fort where winter stood:
    — Only blown and drenching grasses,
    Only rain that never passes,
    Moving mists and sweeping wind,
    And I follow them behind!

October 1912

First published in *The Marlburian*, 31 October 1912.
Line 2: *Court*: the quadrangle, surrounded by classrooms, hall, chapel, and college houses, and intersected by a lime-tree avenue between the gate and C House. This house (to which Sorley belonged) was the old mansion of the Seymours, built in the middle of the seventeenth century, and is the only ancient part of the college buildings.
Line 6: *sweat*: school slang for a run.
Line 21: *Four Miler*, see note on 'J.B.', page 128.

32
A Call to Action

I

A thousand years have passed away,
   Cast back your glances on the scene,
Compare this England of to-day
   With England as she once has been.

Fast beat the pulse of living then:
   The hum of movement, throb of war
The rushing mighty sound of men
   Reverberated loud and far.

They girt their loins up and they trod
   The path of danger, rough and high;
For Action, Action was their god,
   'Be up and doing' was their cry.

A thousand years have passed away;
   The sands of life are running low;
The world is sleeping out her day;
   The day is dying—be it so.

A thousand years have passed amain;
   The sands of life are running thin;
Thought is our leader—Thought is vain;
   Speech is our goddess—Speech is sin.

It needs no thought to understand,
　　No speech to tell, nor sight to see
That there has come upon our land
　　The curse of Inactivity.

We do not see the vital point
　　That 'tis the eighth, most deadly, sin
To wail, 'The world is out of joint'—
　　And not attempt to put it in.

We see the swollen stream of crime
　　Flow hourly past us, thick and wide;
We gaze with interest for a time,
　　And pass by on the other side.

We see the tide of human sin
　　Rush roaring past our very door,
And scarcely one man plunges in
　　To drag the drowning to the shore.

We, dull and dreamy, stand and blink,
　　Forgetting glory, strength and pride,
Half—listless watchers on the brink,
　　Half—ruined victims of the tide.

III

We question, answer, make defence,
　　We sneer, we scoff, we criticize,
We wail and moan our decadence,
　　Enquire, investigate, surmise;

106

We preach and prattle, peer and pry
    And fit together two and two;
We ponder, argue, shout, swear, lie—
    We will not, for we cannot, DO.

Pale puny soldiers of the pen,
    Absorbed in this your inky strife,
Act as of old, when men were men,
    England herself and life yet life.

IV

Soon after lunch we take a chair,
    And light a comforting cigar,
And muse with languid, mild, despair
    Upon the state in which things are.
The shadows lengthen on the wall;
    The evening chill pervades the air;
We may have been asleep—at all
    Events, we still are sitting there!

V

Yes, still we ponder, pry, infer,
    Decide—and do not DO the same;
Still shrink from action, still prefer
    To watch, instead of play, the game.

Still shelter cowering from the storm
    And shrink to save the drowning crew,
And still pay others to perform
    Our duties which we dare not do.

For we have utterly forgot
  One great unanswerable fact:
We are not tools, but craftsmen—not
  Machines to think, but men to Act!

A few have learned the lesson: they
  Can never know the good they do;
They help their brethren on their way,
  They fight and conquer: —all too few.

We, fooled and fooling, must be taught
  That herein lies our greatest need:
That we have let the power of thought
  Impoverish the power of deed!

We must be taught to Act: 'tis vain
  To tear the hair and beat the brow,
Wring dry the thoughts, ransack the brain
  And write—as I am doing now!

October 1912

The first three parts were published in *The Marlburian*,
31 October 1912. The final parts, IV and V, were exclud-
ed from the school magazine, for obvious reasons! They
are published here for the first time.

33
A Tale of Two Careers

I SUCCESS

He does not dress as other men,
   His 'kish' is loud and gay,
His 'side' is as the 'side' of ten
   Because his 'barnes' are grey.

His head has swollen to a size
   Beyond the proper size for heads,
He metaphorically buys
   The ground on which he treads.

Before his face of haughty grace
   The ordinary mortal cowers:
A 'forty-cap' has put the chap
   Into another world from ours.

The funny little world that lies
   'Twixt High Street and the Mound
Is just a swarm of buzzing flies
   That aimlessly go round:

If one is stronger in the limb
   Or better able to work hard,
It's quite amusing to watch him
   Ascending heavenward.

But if one cannot work or play
    (Who loves the better part too well),
It's really sad to see the lad
    Retained compulsorily in hell.

II FAILURE

We are the wasters, who have no
    Hope in this world here, neither fame,
Because we cannot collar low
    Nor write a strange dead tongue the same
As strange dead men did long ago.

We are the weary, who begin
    The race with joy, but early fail,
Because we do not care to win
    A race that goes not to the frail
And humble: only the proud come in.

We are the shadow-forms, who pass
    Unheeded hence from work and play.
We are to-day, but like the grass
    That to-day is, we pass away;
And no one stops to say 'Alas!'

Though we have little, all we have
    We give our School. And no return
We can expect for what we gave;
    No joys; only a summons stern,
'Depart, for others entrance crave!'

As soon as she can clearly prove
    That from us is no hope of gain,
Because we only bring her love
    And cannot bring her strength or brain,
She tells us, 'Go: it is enough.'

She turns us out at seventeen,
    We may not know her any more,
And all our life with her has been
    A life of seeing others score,
While we sink lower and are mean.

We have seen others reap success
    Full-measure. None has come to us.
Our life has been one failure. Yes,
    But does not God prefer it thus?
God does not also praise success.

And for each failure that we meet,
    And for each place we drop behind,
Each toil that holds our aching feet,
    Each star we seek and never find,
God, knowing, gives us comfort meet.

The School we care for has not cared
    To cherish nor keep our names to be
Memorials. God hath prepared
    Some better thing for us, for we
His hopes have known, His failures shared.

November 1912

First published in *The Marlburian*, 11 November 1912.

Line 2: *kish* (pronounced *kĭsh*), a flat cushion which folded double and was used by Marlburians as a book-carrier. The 'bloods' (or athletic aristocrats of the school) affected garish colours (*loud and gay*) for the lining of their kishes.

Line 4: *barnes*, school slang for trousers. The school rules for dress were slightly relaxed for 'bloods'.

Line 11: *forty-cap*, for football, equivalent to about second fifteen—obtained by Sorley a year after these verses were written.

34
Peace

There is silence in the evening when the long days cease,
And a million men are praying for an ultimate release
From strife and sweat and sorrow — they are praying
    for peace
                But God is marching on.

Peace for a people that is striving to be free!
Peace for the children of the wild wet sea!
Peace for the seekers of the promised land — do we
              Want peace when God has none?

We pray for rest and beauty that we know we
    cannot earn,
And ever are we asking for a honey-sweet return;
But God will make it bitter, make it bitter, till we learn
              That with tears the race is run.

And did not Jesus perish to bring to men, not peace,
But a sword, a sword for battle and a sword that
    should not cease?
Two thousand years have passed us. Do we still
    want peace
              Where the sword of Christ has shone?

Yes, Christ perished to present us with a sword,
That strife should be our portion and more strife
    our reward,
For toil and tribulation and the glory of the Lord
              And the sword of Christ are one.

If you want to know the beauty of the thing called rest,
Go, get it from the poets, who will tell you it is best
(And their words are sweet as honey) to lie flat upon
      your chest
                  And sleep till life is gone.

I know that there is beauty where the low streams run,
And the weeping of the willows and the big sunk sun,
But I know my work is doing and it never shall be done,
                  Though I march for ages on.

Wild is the tumult of the long grey street,
O, is it never silent from the tramping of their feet?
Here, Jesus, is Thy triumph, and here the world's defeat,
                  For from here all peace has gone.

There's a stranger thing than beauty in the ceaseless
      city's breast,
In the throbbing of its fever—and the wind is in the west,
And the rain is driving forward where there is no rest,
                  For the Lord is marching on.

December 1912

First published in *The Marlburian*, 19 December 1912.
Professor Sorley suggests that the lines

> I know that there is beauty where the low streams run,
> And the weeping of the willows and the big sunk sun,

'are perhaps the only lines in the book which recall the
scenery of [Sorley's] Cambridge home.'

35
Expectans Expectavi

From morn to midnight, all day through,
I laugh and play as others do,
I sin and chatter, just the same
As others with a different name.

And all year long upon the stage
I dance and tumble and do rage
So vehemently, I scarcely see
The inner and eternal me.

I have a temple I do not
Visit, a heart I have forgot,
A self that I have never met,
A secret shrine — and yet, and yet

This sanctuary of my soul
Unwitting I keep white and whole,
Unlatched and lit, if Thou should'st care
To enter or to tarry there.

With parted lips and outstretched hands
And listening ears Thy servant stands,
Call Thou early, call Thou late,
To Thy great service dedicate.

First published after Sorley's death in *The Times Literary Supplement*, 28 October 1915. The title is taken from

Psalm 40, 'I waited patiently . . .' and was later set to music and sung as an anthem.

Professor Sorley dates this poem May 1915, yet in the original MS at Marlborough College there is no such date, only a note at the top which has been partly obliterated; it looks as though it says 'Written 1912'. If this is so it would explain the entirely uncharacteristic piety of tone, for Sorley had gone through a conventionally religious phase in 1912 (see 'Peace', 'A Call to Action' and 'The Seekers') to which he never returned. It is very likely that his parents wished to represent him as a believer after his death.

36

Verse Letter to the Editor of 'The Marlburian'

Dear Sir, — I write this note in answer
  To Mr Requiem's effusion,
Which simply doesn't give a chance, sir,
  To the intrusion

Of that erection on the Mound, which
  Was built, I'm sure, by first-rate fingers,
That charming chimney, sir, around which
  Sweet music lingers.

It brings us nearer to the life of
  The throbbing, great heart of the nation;
It thrills us with the mighty strife of
  Illiquidation;

The Gods of Progress overcome it,
  The Spirit of the Age is o'er it.
The thing is perfectly consummate,
  I just adore it!

For this asylum here of dunces
  Though quite innocuous (I'm sure all
Your readers will agree at once) is
  Most deadly rural.

But lately, there has been a series
  Of fresh events across our curtain,
Which *do* remind us that the year is
  Turned 1913.

First, once when things were going slower
    Than fitted my idea of heaven,
I looked, and lo! a motor mower
    Crossed the Eleven.

Next, funny red things long have glistened
    On walls; and when the place is blazing,
You simply press a button—isn't
    It most amazing?

(On looking over that last stanza
    I fear it needs some explanation.
I meant those patent kill-fire cans, a
    Great innovation.)

Third on the list (there's nothing like lists)
    Six members of the staff were lately
Discovered to be motor-cyclists,
    Which pained us greatly.

And so we're getting quite progressive
    Since that sweet chimney came among us.
—And yet it could not be liked less if
    The thing had hung us!

For Mr Requiem tries to raise field
    And road and house and town to fight it,
And quotes the everlasting Masefield,
    And gets excited.

These noises, sir, which now make *you* sick,
    (Who see not what a stuffy brute you're

Becoming), are the stirring music
   Of England's future.

The time, the golden time, is coming
   When every tune and song and hymn, nay,
All music, will be like the strumming
   Of this great chimney.

With beauties fading from before us,
   And vast machineries arriving,
And all the world a shrieking chorus
   Of ceaseless striving —

I hail thee, Chimney, who wilt wipe all
   Aesthetic Rot away for ever,
And sign myself —
   A STERN DISCIPLE OF LOUD ENDEAVOUR.

This verse letter to the editor of *The Marlburian* was published on 25 February 1913. It refers to correspondence of 11 February.

37
The River

He watched the river running black
   Beneath the blacker sky;
It did not pause upon its track
   Of silent instancy;
It did not hasten, nor was slack,
   But still went gliding by.

It was so black. There was no wind
   Its patience to defy.
It was not that the man had sinned,
   Or that he wished to die.
Only the wide and silent tide
   Went slowly sweeping by.

The mass of blackness moving down
   Filled full of dreams the eye;
The lights of all the lighted town
   Upon its breast did lie;
The tall black trees were upside down
   In the river phantasy.

He had an envy for its black
   Inscrutability;
He felt impatiently the lack
   Of that great law whereby
The river never travels back
   But still goes gliding by;

But still goes gliding by, nor clings
    To passing things that die,
Nor shows the secrets that it brings
    From its strange source on high.
And he felt 'We are two living things
    And the weaker one is I.'

He saw the town, that living stack
    Piled up against the sky.
He saw the river running black
    On, on and on: O, why
Could he not move along his track
    With such consistency?

He had a yearning for the strength
    That comes of unity:
The union of one soul at length
    With its twin-soul to lie:
To be a part of one great strength
    That moves and cannot die.

                *   *   *

He watched the river running black
    Beneath the blacker sky.
He pulled his coat about his back,
    He did not strive nor cry.
He put his foot upon the track
    That still went gliding by.

The thing that never travels back
    Received him silently.
And there was left no shred, no wrack

To show the reason why:
Only the river running black
Beneath the blacker sky.

February 1913

First published in *The Marlburian*, 25 February 1913.
This poem, as there printed, was preceded by the explan-
ation, 'Early in January a man, without any conceivable
reason for doing so, drowned himself in the —. The
verdict at the inquest was, as is usual in such cases,
"Suicide during temporary insanity". This is the truth.'

38
The Seekers

The gates are open on the road
That leads to beauty and to God.

Perhaps the gates are not so fair,
Nor quite so bright as once they were,
When God Himself on earth did stand
And gave to Abraham His hand
And led him to a better land.

For lo! the unclean walk therein,
And those that have been soiled with sin.
The publican and harlot pass
Along: they do not stain its grass.
In it the needy has his share,
In it the foolish do not err.
Yes, spurned and fool and sinner stray
Along the highway and the way.

And what if all its ways are trod
By those whom sin brings near to God?
This journey soon will make them clean:
Their faith is greater than their sin.

For still they travel slowly by
Beneath the promise of the sky,
Scorned and rejected utterly;
Unhonoured; things of little worth
Upon the highroads of this earth;

Afflicted, destitute and weak:
Nor find the beauty that they seek,
The God they set their trust upon:
— Yet still they march rejoicing on.

March 1913

First published in *The Marlburian*, 13 March 1913.
Line 15: *the highway and the way*, cf. Isaiah xxxv. 8.

39
What You Will

O come and see, it's such a sight,
So many boys all doing right:
To see them underneath the yoke,
Blindfolded by the elder folk,
Move at a most impressive rate
Along the way that is called straight.
O, it is comforting to know
They're in the way they ought to go.
But don't you think it's far more gay
To see them slowly leave the way
And limp and loose themselves and fall?
O, that's the nicest thing of all.
I love to see this sight, for then
I know they are becoming men,
And they are tiring of the shrine
Where things are really not divine.

I do not know if it seems brave
The youthful spirit to enslave,
And hedge about, lest it should grow.
I don't know if it's better so
In the long end. I only know
That when I have a son of mine,
He shan't be made to droop and pine,
Bound down and forced by rule and rod
To serve a God who is no God.
But I'll put custom on the shelf
Ar d make him find his God himself.

Perhaps he'll find him in a tree,
Some hollow trunk, where you can see.
Perhaps the daisies in the sod
Will open out and show him God.
Or will he meet him in the roar
Of breakers as they beat the shore?
Or in the spiky stars that shine?
Or in the rain (where I found mine)?
Or in the city's giant moan?
    — A God who will be all his own,
    To whom he can address a prayer
    And love him, for he is so fair,
    And see with eyes that are not dim
    And build a temple meet for him.

30 June 1913

First published in *The Marlburian*, 10 July 1913.
Line 11: *loose*: thus in all previous editions.

40
J.B.

There's still a horse on Granham hill,
And still the Kennet moves, and still
Four Miler sways and is not still.
    But where is her interpreter?

The downs are blown into dismay,
The stunted trees seem all astray,
Looking for someone clad in grey
    And carrying a golf-club thing;

Who, them when he had lived among,
Gave them what they desired, a tongue.
Their words he gave them to be sung
    Perhaps were few, but they were true.

The trees, the downs, on either hand,
Still stand, as he said they would stand.
But look, the rain in all the land
    Makes all things dim with tears of him.

And recently the Kennet croons,
And winds are playing widowed tunes.
—He has not left our 'toun o' touns,'
    But taken it away with him!

October 1913

First publi hed in *The Marlburian*, 9 October 1913.

J.B. is John Bain, a Marlborough classics master, himself a minor poet. Like Sorley, he was a Scot. This poem is a lament over the departure of Bain, the laureate of the school, who had resigned and left Marlborough at the end of the previous summer term. Sorley's acquaintance with him was entirely an out-of-school one. See note on 'I have not brought my Odyssey' (pp. 133-34).

Line 1: *Granham hill*, on the opposite side of the Kennet from Marlborough College. The *horse* is a rather inferior specimen of the 'white horses' cut out in the chalk, of which there are other and more famous examples in the Wiltshire and Berkshire downs. It was cut by boys of a local private school in 1804.

Line 3: *Four Miler*, the school name for Four Mile Clump, so called because it lies at the fourth milestone on the old Swindon Road; it is in the same direction as Barbury Camp and about a mile short of it.

Line 19: *toun o' touns*, one of several echoes in the poem of John Bain's school songs 'The Scotch Marlburian' and 'All Aboard'.

41
'I have not brought my Odyssey'

I have not brought my Odyssey
With me here across the sea;
But you'll remember, when I say
How, when they went down Sparta way,
To sandy Sparta, long ere dawn
Horses were harnessed, rations drawn,
Equipment polished sparkling bright,
And breakfasts swallowed (as the white
of Eastern heavens turned to gold) —
The dogs barked, swift farewells were told.
The sun springs up, the horses neigh,
Crackles the whip thrice — then away!
From sun-go-up to sun-go-down
All day across the sandy down
The gallant horses galloped, till
The wind across the downs more chill
Blew, the sun sank and all the road
Was darkened, that it only showed
Right at the end of the town's red light
And twilight glimmering into night.

The horses never slackened till
They reached the doorway and stood still.
Then came the knock, the unlading; then
The honey-sweet converse of men,
The splendid bath, the change of dress,
Then — O the grandeur of their Mess,
The henchmen, the prim stewardess!

And O the breaking of old ground,
The tales, after the port went round!
(The wondrous wiles of old Odysseus,
Old Agamemnon and his misuse
Of his command, and that young chit
Paris—who didn't care a bit
For Helen—only to annoy Pa
He did it really, κ.τ.λ.)

But soon they led amidst the din
The honey-sweet ἀοιδός in,
Whose eyes were blind, whose soul had sight,
Who knew the fame of men in fight—
Bard of white hair and trembling foot,
Who sang whatever God might put
Into his heart.
              And there he sung,
Those war-worn veterans among,
Tales of great war and strong hearts wrung,
Of clash of arms, of council's brawl,
Of beauty that must early fall,
Of battle hate and battle joy
By the old windy walls of Troy.
They felt that they were unreal then,
Visions and shadow-forms, not men.
But those the Bard did sing and say
(Some were their comrades, some were they)
Took shape and loomed and strengthened more
Greatly than they had guessed of yore.

And now the fight begins again,
The old war-joy, the old war-pain.

Sons of one school across the sea
We have no fear to fight, for we   59
Have echo of our deeds in you
We have our ἀοιδός too.

And soon, O soon, I do not doubt it,
With the body or without it,
We shall all come tumbling down
To our old wrinkled red-capped town.
Perhaps the road up Ilsley way,   66
The old ridge-track, will be my way.
High up among the sheep and sky,
Look down on Wantage, passing by,
And see the smoke from Swindon town;
And then full left at Liddington,
Where the four winds of heaven meet
The earth-blest traveller to greet.
And then my face is toward the south,
There is a singing on my mouth:
Away to rightward I descry
My Barbury ensconced in sky,
Far underneath the Ogbourne twins,   78
And at my feet the thyme and whins,
The grasses with their little crowns
Of gold, the lovely Aldbourne downs
And that old signpost (well I knew
That crazy signpost, arms askew,
Old mother of the four grass ways).
And then my mouth is dumb with praise,
For, past the wood and chalkpit tiny,
A glimpse of Marlborough ἐρατεινή!   87
So I descend beneath the rail

To warmth and welcome and wassail,
And you, our minstrel, you our bard,
Who makes war's grievous things and hard,
Lightsome and glorious and fair
Will be, at least in spirit, there.
We'll read your rhymes, and we will sing
The toun o' touns till the roofs ring.
And if you'll come among us, then
We shall be most blest of men,
We shall forget the old old pain,
Remember Marlborough again
And hearken all the tales you tell   100
And bless our old ἀοιδός.
                                    Well,
This for the future. Now we stand
Stronger through you, to guard our land,
I do but give the thanks of each
(Thanks far far greater than my speech)
Of those who knew or did not know
(For all knew you) not long ago
In places that we see in sleep
Our eyes are dry but our hearts weep
Warm living tears that memory dear
Calls up the moment that we hear
(For we do hear it) your kind voice
Who understood us, men and boys.
So now and for the ages through
We are all dead and living too.
Our common life lies on your tongue
For as the bards sang, you have sung.

This from the battered trenches—rough,

Jingling and tedious enough.
And so I sign myself to you:
One, who some crooked pathways knew
Round Bedwyn: who could scarcely leave   122
The Downs on a December eve:
Was at his happiest in shorts,
And got—not many good reports!
Small skill of rhyming in his hand—
But you'll forgive—you'll understand.

12 July 1915

First published in *Marlborough and Other Poems*, January 1916.
This verse epistle was originally sent to John Bain (see note on 'J.B.', page 129). Bain discovered the authorship by sending the envelope in which it came to a Marlborough master, and then replied:

From far away there comes a Voice,
   Singing its song across the sea—
A song to make man's heart rejoice—
   Of Marlborough and the Odyssey.

A Voice that sings of Now and Then,
   Of minstrel joys and tiny towns,
Of flowering thyme and fighting men,
   Of Sparta's sands and Marlborough's Downs.

God grant, dear Voice, one day again
   We see those Downs in April weather,
And snuff the breeze and smell the rain,
   And stand in C House Porch together.

Bain allowed Professor Sorley to print Sorley's epistle to him, with the exception of two passages (lines 59-61 and 90-118 above) which he felt were too flattering. The missing lines were first published in the Literary Supplement to *The Marlburian*, Lent term 1967. The poem is given here in its entirety.

Line 35, κ.τ.λ. και τα λοιπα: etcetera.

Line 37, ἀοιδός: minstrel.

Line 66, *Ilsley*: about twenty miles due east of Swindon and on the northern slope of the Berkshire downs.

Line 78, *the Ogbourne twins*: Ogbourne St George and Ogbourne St Andrew, villages in the Valley of the Og, about five and three miles respectively north of Marlborough.

Line 81, *Aldbourne downs*: on the eastern side of the Og and adjoining the Marlborough downs.

Line 87, ἐρατεινή: lovely.

Line 122, *Bedwyn*: Great and Little Bedwyn, about a mile from the south-eastern corner of Savernake forest and about six miles from Marlborough.

42

'It was spring'

It was spring. And we hoped in the spring
　　For a glorious summer.
And the summer came, yes, good old thing!
　　But we found the new-comer

Was bright but in days of hope gone,
　　But approaching (poor harlot)
Threw us tattered raiment to don
　　And gave others the scarlet.

So this is the end of it all!
　　Of the sloth and the slumber,
Of the hates that we hated like gall,
　　And the loves, few in number.

And no one will now Pity say
　　Or can back again wish us,
Who have done nothing good in our day,
　　And (what's worse) nothing vicious.

We have fought for ourselves like black Hell,
　　But, since we were our standard,
Does it matter we have not fought well
　　And weak failed, where we planned hard?

The time made us Outcast and Dunce,
    Though for Kingship intended.
It might have been beautiful — once!
    But now it is ended.

December 1913

First published in *The Letters of Charles Sorley* (Cambridge University Press, 1919).

The poem was sent by Sorley to his friend A.E. Hutchinson, 14 November 1914, with the words 'You may be interested in the following verses I wrote on the last night [at Marlborough], while miserably struggling with innumerable packing-cases in the void of an empty, swept and garnished study'.

43

Questions Expecting the Answer Yes
Addressed to A.E.H.

I wonder, does that ancient bell still clang
    Welcome to new arrivals every day,
As up the hill and round, a small black gang
    With their inevitable coffin stray,
    Decked out in black, with flowers in white array,
And suitable stiff hats and heads that hang,
    And downcast eyes with ruts where tears have been,
    And all those other things which make Death mean?

And some strange sweaty creatures stop to see
    On those bald heights—strange bare-kneed passers-by,
With scarves about their necks that they may be
    (Do they still think it?) comely to the eye,
    And say, In Marlborough they daily die,
And gape and pass on downwards to brew tea.
    And having downward passed, do they still find
    A mimic city filled with men who mind?

Still haunt blear bearded men, whose eyes are ill,
    The basements? Does the man without a name
Still ride his washing waggon down the hill
    Into the laundry? Is it still his game
    To make in Court disturbance with the same?
And do the Widow and the Curate still   22
    Get up at Vosse's, and go straight to cold,
    And feed on Lyall's syrup coloured gold?

And on the Common is there still mock war,
    Where many minds are sacrificed to one

Small Ball, and talk of it, not sorry for
    Their meaningless behaviour? Is this done
    Still? Do they still care whether they have won?
And is there still a Folly called the Corps
    Allowed out twice a week and thinking then
    It's learning how to kill its fellow-men?

On Sundays are there thirty chosen ones
    Who wear white ties, because their lives are white,
Who spurn the Wrong, nor eat Duck's damp cream buns,
    But eat fair Knapton's cakes, and choose the Right?
    And do they still on Saturdays at night
Put out all best clothes ready, tons and tons,
    For Sunday wear, because the Lord likes best
    To see his faithful worshippers well-dressed?

And say, is Classroom changed into a den
    Of bright-faced British youth that nobly tries
To follow in the steps of those great men
    Who always fig-leaves wear, or made-up ties,
    And sacrifice their lives to Exercise,

And clench their fists and feed on Force, and when
    Worn out by muscular and manly toil
    Read chapters from clean, Christian, Conan Doyle?

And is there still a refuge, when each day
    The same small life, the same poor problems brings?
Is there still change? O, is there still a way
    Outward, across those many earth-risings,

A Comfort, and a place to find new things?
And are the downs, and are the downs still grey?
And is the Chapel still a house of sin
Where smiling men let false Religion in?

[N.B. Verse vi hopes for the Answer No.]

First published in *The Letters of Charles Sorley* (Cambridge University Press, 1919).

Sorley wrote these verses on Marlborough while living in Schwerin with the Beutins and sent them to his friend Alan Hutchinson on 7 February 1914. 'I enclose a piece of verse,' he told Hutchinson, 'which I composed through sheer boredom on the Kaiser's birthday . . .'.

Lines 22-23: *The Widow and the Curate* are names which he gave to two types of boy; *Vosse's* is the first bell in the morning; to *go straight to cold* is to take a cold bath without first washing in warm water.

Line 34: Prefects wore white ties on a Sunday.

Lines 35-36: *Duck . . . Knapton* were the names of Marlborough College's two rival tuckshops.

44
'Women who seek, obtain, employ Divorce'

Women who seek, obtain, employ Divorce
Are only fit for men of Greed and Force.
Women who take their Breakfast three hours late
Are only fit for men of Spite and Hate.
Women who wear a Tea-gown all the time
Are only fit for men of Vice and Crime.
But women such as get Divorced, and then
Come down to Break their Fast at e-lev-en,
Garbed in a Tea-gown (ye Commandments Ten!)
—Are only fit for Literary Men!

First published in *The Letters of Charles Sorley* (Cambridge University Press, 1919).
Sorley wrote these verses while living in Schwerin and sent them to A.E. Hutchinson on 20 March 1914. They were inspired by Hutchinson's news that Robert Louis Stevenson's wife had just died. Sorley had gained an unfavourable impression of Mrs Stevenson, after hearing from one of her friends that 'she always came down to breakfast at 11 o'clock in a (sigh)—teagown! and besides she was divorced from her first husband'.

45
Quis Desiderio

Check not thy tears, nor be ashamed to sorrow
    For one so dear. Sing us a plaintive song,
O Muse, who from thy sire the lute didst borrow—
    The lute and notes melodious and strong.

So will he wake again from slumber never?
    O, when will Purity, to Justice dear,
Faith unalloyed and Truth unspotted ever,
    When will these virtues ever find his peer?

For him the tears of noble men are flowing,
    But thine, O Virgil, bitterest of all!
Thou prayest God to give him back, not knowing
    He may not, cannot hearken to thy call.

For if thy lyre could move the forests, swelling
    More sweetly than the Thracian bard's of old,
His soul could not revisit its old dwelling;
    For now among the dead he is enrolled

By Mercury, all deaf to supplication,
    Obdurate, gathering all with ruthless rod.
'Tis hard; but Patience lightens Tribulation
    When to remove it is denied by God.

Sorley's translation of Horace, *Odes*, 1, 24, which was
first published in the fourth edition of *Marlborough and*

Other Poems in May 1919, was found in one of his school notebooks. It was this translation which so impressed Geoffrey Bickersteth, then a young master at Marlborough, that he decided to start the Junior Literary Society for him in October 1911.

Index of First Lines of Poems